THE
FIRST EARL
CADOGAN

THE
FIRST EARL
CADOGAN
1672–1726

ROBERT PEARMAN

Haggerston Press

LONDON

© Robert Pearman 1988

First published 1988
by the Haggerston Press
38 Kensington Place, London W8 7PR

Typeset by Fakenham Photosetting Ltd,
Fakenham, Norfolk
Printed in Great Britain
by Redwood Burn Ltd, Trowbridge

1 869812 02 6

Contents

For Penny and Katie

Foreword

My acquaintance with the 1st Earl Cadogan came about when I wrote *The Cadogan Estate*, a general history of both the family and its estate in London. Cadogan was born the son of an Irish lawyer in 1672 and, after education at Westminster School and Trinity College, Dublin, he joined the English army and rose to become its Commander-in-Chief. He fought at the battle of the Boyne and served throughout the long years of the War of the Spanish Succession in the combined roles of Quartermaster-General, Chief-of-Staff and Director of Intelligence to the Duke of Marlborough who became his close friend and patron. Many books have been written about the Duke and his undoubted military prowess but not one has been devoted to his 'alter-ego'[1] without whom, perhaps, Marlborough would not have achieved as much as he did. Certainly the two had a hand-in-glove relationship during the campaigns in Flanders and it is impossible to look in depth at either one of them throughout those years without making copious references to the other.

In addition to his army career Cadogan was also at various times a member of both Houses of Parliament and an Ambassador. Honours were heaped upon him, he amassed enormous personal wealth, and at the peak of his power he occupied a magnificent mansion in Berkshire with houses in London, an estate in Ireland and a castle in Holland. He was an inveterate gambler and letter-writer, a linguist and a man of considerable ambition both for himself and his family. Cadogan was one of those larger-than-life figures that occasionally stride across the stage of history and why he has been overlooked by past and present biographers is a mystery to me. I hope that this modest volume will go some small way to redress the balance.

LONDON   *Robert Pearman*
February 1987

METHOD OF DATING

Until 1752 dates in England and on the Continent differed, owing to our delay in adopting the Reformed Calendar of Gregory XIII. The dates which prevailed in England were known as Old Style, those abroad as New Style. In the seventeenth century the difference was ten days, in the eighteenth century eleven days. Thus, the 1st January 1601(O.S.) was the 11th January 1601(N.S.) and the 1st January 1701(O.S.) was the 12th January 1701(N.S.). All dates that follow should be regarded as New Style unless indicated as Old Style.

It was also customary at this time in English official documents to date the year as beginning on the 25th March. What we should call the 1st January 1700 was then called the 1st January 1699 and so on, for all days up to the 25th March when the year 1700 began. In this book, to avoid confusion the modern practice has been adopted.

[8]

' 'Tis Ireland gives England her soldiers, her generals too.'

George Meredith (1828–1909),
Diana of the Crossways.

Origins

The Cadogan family is descended in male line from Cuhelyn, Prince of Fferlys and his son Elstan Glodrydd, a chieftain of Radnorshire who founded the fifth of the Royal Tribes of Wales. Little is known on any good authority of either father or son apart from the fact that they both lived at or about the turn of the millennium. Given the social structures of the time they would certainly have been fighting men, a supposition which is supported by a translation of the Celtic 'Cadogan' into 'Battle-Keenness'.

Elstan Glodrydd had one son Cadwgan (the family name was later Anglicized although the pronounciation is essentially the same) who was rather more prolific, with three sons called Idnerth of Malienydd, Goronwy and Llewelyn. Cadwgan was used as a baptismal name until the late eighteenth century.

The modern family line springs from Llewelyn, who was slain in 1099 in a border feud, and until 1548 one can only speculate as to how these particular Cadogans lived. It seems reasonably certain from the available evidence that Llewelyn's descendants would have closely allied themselves to the general cause of the Cadogan family as a whole, namely the protection of the family lands both from the Norman invaders and, later, the Marcher barons.

Idnerth had one son Madog who, before his death in 1140, appears to have been a very active warrior and indeed a very active father, siring five sons. The eldest sons, Hywel and Cadwgan, both died in battle in 1142. The third son Marredud fared little better and he was killed by a Marcher Lord, Hugh Mortimer, in 1146. Madog's remaining sons, great nephews of Llewelyn, were longer lived. Cadwallon ruled as Prince of Maelienydd and Ceri while Einion Clud ruled as Prince of Elfael. Their lands which lay 'between the upper waters of the Wye and the Severn' are today located in the County of Powys; Malienydd and Ceri to the north-east close to Llandrindod Wells with Elfael to the south-east in the Painscastle area. Cadwallon had two sons: Maelgwn who died in 1197 and Hywel. Einion Clud's union was similarly blessed with two sons called Einion o'r Porth who died in 1191 and the more prosaically named Walter.

During a visit to Wales in 1187 by the Archbishop of Canterbury, who was intent upon raising a body of crusaders, it appears that among the 3000 well-armed men who donned the cross were Maelgwn and his cousin Einion, although whether they ever reached the Holy Land is unknown. At some time prior to 1197 Cadwallon's sons were deprived of a substantial part of their patrimony in Ceri and Maelienydd when invaders seized the family castle at Cymaron and with the death of Einion o'r Porth the lands in Elfael were also lost, so that by the end of the twelfth century the family's fortunes were very much on the wane.

The Cadogans then drop from view until one Cadwgan ap William appears in 1548, living with his wife Catherine and their three sons at a farmhouse further south in Trostry Fach in Monmouthshire. Cadwgan ap William had three

Oliver Cromwell   *Thomas Wentworth, 1st Earl of Strafford*

grandsons, Cadwgan ap William Cadwgan who died in 1647, Henry Cadogan and the youngest, John Cadogan. Lower Trostre passed from eldest son to eldest son until it was sold in 1670. It seems likely that Henry, being a younger son, needed a good dowry and this he appears to have achieved by marrying Catherine, daughter of Thomas Stradling of Glamorgan, nephew of Sir Thomas Stradling of St Donat's Castle also in Glamorgan. Henry and Catherine had a son named William, born at Cardiff in 1600 during the reign of Queen Elizabeth I. After a period as a soldier of fortune, he went to Ireland in 1633 as a private secretary to Thomas Wentworth, the ill-fated Earl of Strafford, who had been appointed Lord Deputy by Charles I. As a secretary to the Earl, William was well placed both to learn the art of political in–fighting from the older statesman and to benefit from his patronage, as did other members of the Lord Deputy's personal entourage. Their relationship lasted eight years until Lord Strafford was beheaded on Tower Hill on the 12th May 1641. It is during the aftermath that William next appears, as a member of the Irish House of Commons sitting as a 'New English' representative for the borough of Monaghan on a committee seeking to impeach certain of the newly deceased Lord Deputy's former associates. Earlier in 1641 William's first wife Elizabeth Thring of Drogheda had died and the following year he married Elizabeth Roberts of Caenarvon who in that same year gave birth to their only son, Henry.

On the 24th October 1641 the indigenous Catholic Irish rose in revolt against their Protestant rulers who promptly withdrew into their walled towns and planter castles to await the relief belatedly provided by Oliver Cromwell in 1649. These were troubled times in Ireland with savagery

Execution of Strafford

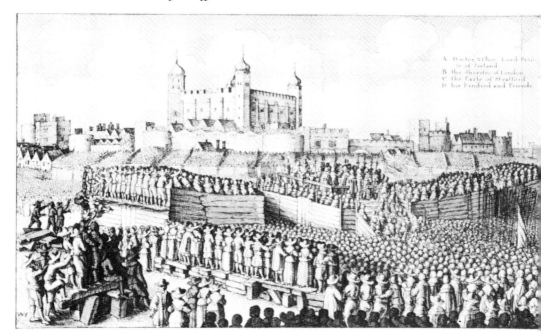

on both sides and so it is not surprising to find William Cadogan holding a commission from Charles I as an army officer. Captain Cadogan was evidently held in some regard by his superiors and shortly afterwards he is recorded as the Deputy Governor of the Castle of Trim in County Antrim. Eventually, however, William, like many another military leader, forsook the Royalist cause with its ambivalent approach to the Catholic rebels and he then appears, having attained his majority, in Cromwell's army.

General Cromwell, defender of the English Commonwealth, landed in Ireland with his main army in August 1649, some six months after the execution of Charles I. He remained nine months, leading his New Model Army on a crusade against the rebels; the massacres at Drogheda and Wexford are well documented. When Cromwell departed, the uprising had effectively ended although a further ten years were to pass before the country was administratively quiet. This broadly coincided with the Restoration of Charles II and with the death on the 14th March 1660 of Major William Cadogan at the age of fifty-nine. For his services he had been appointed Governor of the Castle and Borough of Trim, and he had become again a member of the Irish Parliament. At the time of his demise, he was a man of property with a town house in St George's Lane, Dublin and a country estate at Liscartan in County Meath.

Major Cadogan's will was destroyed along with many other documents during the civil war in Ireland 1922–23. From an earlier extract however it is known that the principal beneficiaries were his wife Elizabeth and his son Henry, then a law student at Trinity College, Dublin. Elizabeth survived William by only five years and her will

Trim Castle

does exist. It has, as might be expected a genteel rustic quality, taking care of the servants and disposing of the livestock, and the 'lands, tenements and hereditaments' are bequeathed to 'my dearly beloved son Mr. Henry Cadogan'. Henry lived in Dublin and he married Bridget Waller, a daughter of Sir Hardress Waller, one of the signatories of the death-warrant of Charles I. Henry Cadogan appears to have had a successful career in the law being at one time the High Sheriff of County Meath. He substantially increased the family acreage, adding an estate in County Limerick which included an early thirteenth-century castle at Adare. The Irish adventure had restored the family's fortune.

CHAPTER II

Formative Years

Henry and Bridget Cadogan had five children of whom William, the eventual 1st Earl Cadogan, was the second eldest son. Although there is no baptismal record of his birth either at the Liscartan parish church or Christ Church Cathedral in Dublin, it is generally held that he was born early in 1672. William's eldest brother Ambose held a commission in the army as a second lieutenant but died a young man in 1693, and his younger brother Charles was born in 1685. He had two sisters: Frances who died when she was only nine years old and Penelope.

William was sent for his education to Westminster School in London, within the shadow of Westminster Abbey. Henry Cadogan's choice of school for William is interesting as Westminster School was usually thought of at the time as more appropriate for those boys destined for a career in the church. The precise date of his entry into the school is unknown although boys generally attended from the age of seven to fifteen years. The regime at Westminster was harsh especially for those boys who were obliged to reside in school. A typical day began at half past five in the morning with ablutions and prayers, followed by lessons from six until breakfast at eight o'clock. Lessons were then resumed until four o'clock in the afternoon. There were no classrooms and the boys were taught in the great school hall, divided into groups called 'forms' after the benches on which they sat. Punishments which were not uncommon were by way of floggings, as a rule administered in front of the whole school. A flogging would, for example, be incurred by any boy who spoke English in the school as opposed to the taught languages of Latin and Greek; a strong incentive for the young scholars to quickly master the ancient tongues. At six o'clock each evening the school was locked-up and discipline then rested in the hands of the older boys. There was a robust system of fagging and no doubt the weaker boys suffered accordingly.

During William's time at Westminster the headmaster was Dr Richard Busby, a redoubtable flogger of both men and boys and a linguist of repute. The tale is told of Busby that one afternoon while in the library he was startled by the crashing of a stone through the window. He immediately despatched a monitor to find the culprit who returned with

Dr Richard Busby

a fashionably dressed young Frenchman who had been watching the boys at play in the school yard quite innocently. Mischievously he had been pointed out to the monitor by the perpetrator of the outrage, a local town boy. Busby gave six of the best to the unfortunate man who, the following morning, sent Busby a note by the hand of his footman challenging the headmaster to a duel. Busby took this in his stride and administered to the struggling servant a birching of double the usual school punishment. The limping footman duly returned to his master who, in the realisation of having met his match, immediately took passage for his own more civilised country.

The boys usually returned home for only six weeks during the course of the year. Life at a public school at this time and indeed later was hard but any suffering that was involved was thought by the parents of the day to be necessary character-forming stuff for the nation's future rulers. The strong survived and the weak went to the wall. The historian Edward Gibbon who attended Westminster sixty years later under a not dissimilar discipline wrote in connection with the public school philosophy that 'a boy of

The Scholars' Dormitory, Westminster School (demolished 1758)

spirit may acquire a praevious and practical experience of the World', and further that, 'In a free intercourse with his equals the habits of truth, fortitude and prudence will insensibly be matured'. If later personal characteristics, aptitudes and physical stature are used as a basis for judgement, it would seem highly likely that the heavily built William would have survived his years at Westminster well, to return to Ireland in 1687 a tall self-reliant and self-confident young man of fifteen years, there to continue his studies at Trinity College, Dublin, the Alma Mater of his father Henry Cadogan. The years spent in England would have softened William's Irish accent but doubtless some intonation would always remain to mark him as a man from across the Irish Sea.

In 1685, during William's time at Westminster, Charles II had died, to be succeeded by his brother James II. Unlike his brother, James was an unpopular overt Roman Catholic and in the year of his accession he appointed his friend Richard Talbot, the Catholic Earl of Tyrconnell, Lieutenant-General of the Irish army on the understanding that he would purge the officer element of the Anglo-Irish Protestants. While James repeatedly affirmed his support for the Act of Settlement 1662, which perpetuated minority rule in Ireland, his general policy of Catholicisation in the army and administration and his Declarations of Indulgence suspending the laws against Catholics and dissenters in the end alienated every important section of opinion in Protestant England. The birth of his son in June 1688 and the possibility of a Catholic succession proved to be the catalyst which led seven leading statesmen, both Whigs and Tories, to invite the intervention of the Protestant William of Orange, Stadtholder of Holland, a grandson of Charles I, and husband to James's daughter Mary. (The Whigs were members of an English political group formed during the reign of Charles II who wanted to exclude from the throne any Roman Catholic monarch and limit the power of the Crown. The Tories were those of a contrary view, some of whom, notwithstanding, were prepared to support the invitation extended to William of Orange. Most Tories favoured the Stuart cause after 1689 but by the time George III came to the throne in 1760 they supported the established monarchy. The Whigs were succeeded by the Liberals in the mid-nineteenth century.)

William of Orange landed at Torbay in November 1688, issued a declaration promising to defend the liberties of England and the Protestant religion and to call a free Parliament and then marched unopposed to London. James hereupon took ship to France and by this act he was deemed to have abdicated. Thus came about the 'Glorious Revolution' which proved to be a landmark in English constitutional history. It ensured through the Bill of Rights in 1689 that no Roman Catholic would ever again be the Sovereign, that Englishmen possessed inviolate civic and political rights and it ensured, further, the political supremacy of Parliament. William III and his queen, Mary II, accepted these conditions on ascending the throne in April of the same year.

During these momentous events the young Cadogan continued with his studies at Trinity College, possibly with a view to following in his father's footsteps, but eventually the flight of King James was to have a dramatic effect on his life and cause him to change from aspiring lawyer to ambitious soldier. For a spirited and physically well-developed young man with warrior's lineage, the metamorphosis probably came like a breath of fresh air: away with the books and on with the sword.

Having established himself in France, James sought the help of Louis XIV to regain his English throne. James's supporters, the Jacobites, were, not surprisingly, at their strongest in Ireland and so James disembarked from a French ship at Kinsale in March 1689 backed by troops and arms supplied by King Louis. James was given generous support by the indigenous Catholic population and soon the country was under his control with the exception of Derry and Enniskillen in the north. In August 1689, King William's forces opened a campaign against the Irish Jacobites who in the following month ejected the fellows and students from Trinity College, which they then proceeded to use as a barracks and prison. There seemed little doubt that a permanent Jacobite administration in Ireland would cause the Protestant Cadogan family to lose their estates in County Meath and County Limerick and accordingly William's way was clear: he joined the Protestant forces. Two new regiments were raised in Ireland in 1689 to aid King William; Brigadier-General Thomas Erle's Regiment

Trinity College, Dublin as it was in Cadogan's time

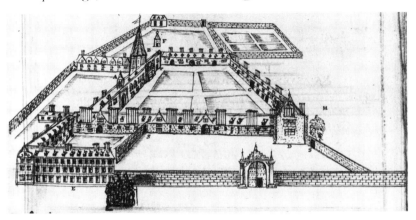

The Battle of the Boyne

of Foot and that into which Cadogan was commissioned as cornet: Colonel Wynne's Enniskillen Dragoons.

In mid-June 1690, King William arrived in Ireland with reinforcements and took overall command of an army of 36,000 men which included Dutch, Danish and Huguenot troops. In a wider context this Protestant army saw itself as fighting the might of France. After reviewing his army King William marched towards the Irish capital, causing the Jacobites to fall back until they reached the south bank of the river Boyne some thirty miles north of Dublin, where James decided to make a stand with his generally inferior army of 25,000 men. The battle of the Boyne was fought on the 11th July and there seemed little doubt as to the outcome. The Jacobite army was routed and within three weeks James had returned to France leaving his son-in-law to consolidate the conquest of Ireland. William Cadogan distinguished himself at the Boyne and now, at the age of 18, he was embarked on a remarkable career.

CHAPTER III

From Cornet to Quartermaster-General

John Churchill, the future 1st Duke of Marlborough, whose own career was to have such signal effect upon William Cadogan's, was born in Devonshire in May 1650. His father Sir Winston, a lawyer like Henry Cadogan, was appointed a Commissioner for Irish Land Claims in 1662 and in that same year he removed with his family to Dublin where John attended school. Given the circumstances obtaining in Ireland at the time, it is quite likely that the Cadogan and Churchill families became known to one another and certainly at a later date their Dublin experiences would have been useful common ground between the older Churchill and the younger Cadogan. Churchill's military career began in 1668 with volunteer service in Tangiers and he soldiered thereafter constantly and successfully in Europe through to the battle of Sedgemoor in 1685 which ended Monmouth's Rebellion. Under the patronage of James II, Churchill was ennobled as Baron Churchill in that same year which also saw him confirmed in his appointment as Colonel of the King's Own Regiment of Dragoons. Three years later in 1688 Lord Churchill, a devout Protestant, severed his ties with King James and swore

John Churchill, 1st Duke of Marlborough

allegiance to William of Orange. In the ensuing coronation honours Lord Churchill was created Earl of Marlborough and, with the rank of lieutenant-general, was given the task of reorganising the English army and undoing the harm done by James's Catholic appointees.

Lord Marlborough took no part in the early military campaign in Ireland during which King William had been content to rely upon his Dutch generals. Marlborough's mind however had not been idle and he formulated a plan for the seizure of the vital southern Irish ports of Cork and Kinsale which, if successful, would isolate the remaining Jacobite forces in Ireland for an eventual mopping-up operation. After some hesitation on the part of his other generals, the king approved the plan and Marlborough successfully laid siege to the ports in October 1690. It was during the attacks upon the two ports that the merits of William Cadogan as a soldier first attracted the attention of Marlborough, although another ten years were to pass before the great commander was to promote Cadogan onto his staff. In the meantime the young Cadogan set about learning in greater depth the profession of arms by fighting with the English army in that part of present-day France, Belgium and Holland then known as Flanders, against the old enemy, France, in the war of the League of Augsberg. The war had begun in 1688 and England was part of a Grand Alliance formed with the Holy Roman Empire and the United Provinces to halt France's expansionist plans. The Empire was a confederation of states including Austria, Hanover, Prussia and Bavaria ruled by an elected Emperor, in practice always a member of the Hapsburg family. The United Provinces were the northern Netherlands, known in England simply as Holland. The war which began with a phoney period, ground on for seven years before it came to an inconclusive end in 1697 with the peace of Ryswick, by which time Cadogan had been commissioned in General Erle's Regiment of Foot with the rank of captain. During the ensuing year he returned to his old regiment, now known as the Inniskilling Dragoons, as Quartermaster with the rank of major.

Major Cadogan at the age of 26 had grown to become a 'giant'[1] of a man; judging from portraits of him in his mature years he was some six feet six inches tall, weighing in the order of fifteen stone. He is portrayed bewigged with a bold face touched with arrogance and with a straight nose, full dark eyes and a well modelled mouth: a cavalryman built to create fear in the heart of the enemy and to encourage respect from his own men. At the conclusion of hostilities Cadogan settled down to peace-time soldiering, suspecting no doubt that it would not be too long before he would be called to action again, given the inconclusiveness of the recent conflict.

After a period of disfavour, Lord Marlborough was now once again restored in William's royal esteem. Queen Mary had died in 1694 and in August 1700 the infant Duke of Gloucester, born in 1689 and heir apparent to the future Queen Anne, died from smallpox. This gave rise to the Act of Settlement in 1701 which vested the royal succession in the descendants of Sophia of Hanover, granddaughter of James I, in the event of William and Anne dying without heirs. William died the following year without issue leaving Princess Anne, sister of the late Queen Mary, to be enthroned in March 1702.

[27]

Prior to William's death there was set in train a sequence of events that was to lead to another war in mainland Europe, the War of the Spanish Succession which proved to be the last and bloodiest of the wars fought against Louis XIV. Spain was ruled, until his death in November 1700, by the childless and impotent Charles II and his European domain also included Milan, Naples, Sicily and the Spanish Netherlands. These last were the southern part of the Netherlands which in greater part and together with part of the old Bishopric of Liége became Belgium in 1830. Spain's overseas possessions encompassed Mexico, Peru, Florida and the Phillipines. The question as to who would succeed Charles was therefore a very important one for the other European powers. There were three claimants to the Spanish crown: the French Dauphin, Louis' son and heir; the Archduke Charles of Austria; and Joseph Ferdinand, Electoral Prince of Bavaria. In 1698 and 1699 Partition Treaties were negotiated between the interested parties by William and Louis and the territorial division envisaged seemed to provide a solution. Unfortunately, however, their grand designs came to naught when Charles II made a will on his deathbed naming the 16-year-old Philip of Anjou, Louis' grandson, his sole heir. There was thus a danger of the French and Spanish crowns uniting to present a formidable power bloc and it was with this prospect in view that the by now ailing William decided that Marlborough must play a greater rôle on the national scene. On the 31st May 1701 he was appointed commander of all the English foot already serving in Holland and on the 28th June, he was appointed to that country as Ambassador Extraordinary and Plenipotentiary with the right to 'conceive treaties without reference, if needs be, to King or Parliament'.[2]

Cloaked with his new powers, Marlborough sought to have on his staff only those men of high ability and trust-worthiness who were personally known to him. Accordingly on the 1st June 1701 Cadogan, now aged 29, was given a brevet promotion to Colonel of Foot, followed on the 1st July by a commission as Quartermaster-General, adding later to this rôle those of Marlborough's Chief-of-Staff and Director of Intelligence. Colonel Cadogan, his star now in the ascendant, accompanied his commander and William to Holland in July and duly took up his duties. Negotiations by Marlborough with the French proved inconclusive and it soon became apparent that all that could be hoped for was to make another alliance to fight *Le Roi Soleil*. French troops had by this time been sent, in the name of Philip of Anjou, into the Spanish Netherlands and the Bishopric of Liége. By the beginning of 1702 a second Grand Alliance had been entered into by England with the United Provinces, and the Empire (excluding Bavaria). France meanwhile had allied herself with Spain, Portugal, Bavaria and Savoy.

An event which was to touch upon Cadogan's later career was the death in France on the 16th September 1701 of the former King James II followed by Louis' recognition of his son James, the Old Pretender, as the lawful King of England. Some six months later King William III died as the result of a riding accident. Anne duly became queen and, in view of her friendship with the Churchill family, Marlborough's appointments were doubly secured. It was against this background that England, on the 15th May 1702, formally declared war on France.

[29]

CHAPTER IV

The War of the Spanish Succession – The Opening Years

The first campaign in 1702 was fought in and around the Bishopric of Liége, allied to the Franco–Spanish cause, and it was generally successful for the Allies although on two occasions near-certain victory was thrown away due to the unwillingness of the Dutch to commit their troops to action. Nevertheless the Allied forces, now under the command of Captain-General Marlborough, did succeed in taking Venlo on the Meuse in September and Stevenswaert and Ruremonde the following month. At Venlo many of the French garrison were put to the sword and at one time in the siege sixty-seven 24-pounder cannon and one hundred and forty mortars were in use against the defenders: a very testing time for Quartermaster-General Cadogan and his staff. In October, the city of Liége was also taken by the Allies before the troops moved into their winter quarters. Campaigning generally in northern Europe at this time did not take place between the months of November and April due to flooding rivers and poor food and forage supplies.

Cadogan's first campaign as Quartermaster-General was

a personal success and at the end of the year Marlborough, now raised to ducal rank by Queen Anne, requested the Paymaster-General of Her Majesty's Forces in the Low Countries to make out a Warrant for £175.4s to Colonel Cadogan '. . . which same Her Majesty is graciously pleased to allow him in consideration of his extraordinary charge, care and pains in the execution of his said office of Quartermaster-General during the last campaign'. As well as a mark of distinction, this was a handsome bonus for Cadogan whose daily rate of pay as Quartermaster-General was ten shillings. (To arrive at a 1987 equivalent for this and other money sums they must be multiplied by forty-two, according to Bank of England statistics.) On the 2nd March 1703 came further royal recognition when Cadogan, no doubt on Marlborough's recommendation, was appointed to the colonelcy of the Sixth Horse, thereafter known as 'Cadogan's Horse'. The regiment was in Ireland at the time and Cadogan sent orders to his second-in-command 'to turn out the little men and unserviceable horse, to enable the Captains to recruit'. Small wonder that Cadogan's Horse eventually gained the reputation as 'Big men mounted on big horses'.[1]

The year of 1703 was to see the Alliance enlarged by the inclusion of Savoy and Portugal who for financial reasons decided to defect from the cause of France and Spain. Although Marlborough had returned to the Hague on the 17th March it was not until mid-August that, following the loss of the battle of Eckeren north of Antwerp at the beginning of the previous month, the Allies gained ground by capturing Huy. In September, Marlborough then invested Limburg some thirty-five miles to the north-east and

THE WAR OF THE SPANISH SUCCESSION: MAIN THEATRE

Miles
0 5 10 15 20 25

Kilometres
0 10 20 30 40

NORTH SEA

The Hague
Utrecht
Arnhem
Rhine
Rotterdam
Brill
ZEELAND
Sluys
Gertruidenburg
Meuse

UNITED PROVINCES

Eindhoven
SPANISH GUELDERLAND
Venlo
Bedburg
Ruremonde
Stevensweaert
Aix-la-Chapelle
Limburg
Maastricht
St Trond
Tongres
Jaar
Corswaren
Liège
Huy
Merdorp
Namur
Meuse

BISHOP OF LIÈGE

Ostend
Dunkirk
To Calais
Wynendael
Canal
Bruges
Ghent
FLANDERS
Lys
Ypres
Menin
Messines
Helchin
Courtrai
Oudenarde
Gavre
Ninove
Lessines
Herfelingen
Hal
Anderlecht
Brussels
Louvain
Corbeck
Meldert
Elixhem
Ramillies
Soignies
Ath
Dender
Denain
Haine
Mons
Malplaquet
Bavai
Espierre

SPANISH NETHERLANDS

Eckeren
Antwerp

FRANCE
Lille
Douai
Bouchain
Cambrai
Scarpe
Béthune
Arleux
Arras
Deule
ARTOIS
HAINAULT

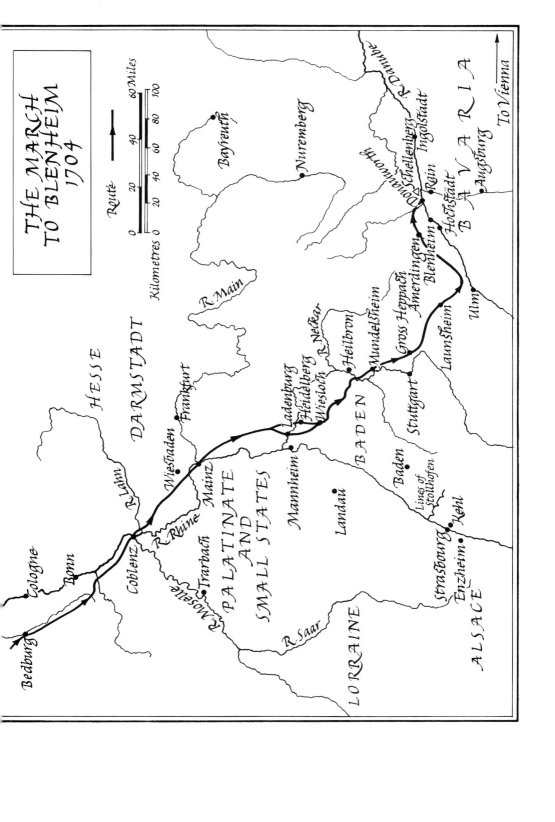

THE MARCH
TO BLENHEIM
1704

Route

Miles
0   20   40   60 Miles

Kilometres
0   20   40   60   80   100

Cologne
Bonn
Bedburg
Coblenz
R. Lahn
R. Rhine
R. Moselle
Trarbach
R. Saar
Mainz
Wiesbaden
Frankfurt
R. Main

HESSE
DARMSTADT
PALATINATE
AND
SMALL STATES

Ladenburg
Heidelberg
Wiesloch
Mannheim
Landau
R. Neckar
Heilbron

BADEN

Baden
Lines of
Stollhofen
Strasbourg
Kehl
Enzheim

ALSACE
LORRAINE

Stuttgart
Mundelsheim
Gross Heppach
Launsheim
Amerdingen
Blenheim
Hochstädt
Donauwörth
Schellenberg
Rain
Ingolstadt
Augsburg
Ulm
R. Danube

BAVARIA

To Vienna

Bayreuth
Nuremberg

twenty miles from Liége, whilst the main army encamped at St Trond. It was from here that Cadogan wrote on the 20th September to his friend Brigadier Lord Raby, great-nephew of the late Earl of Strafford and Envoy to Berlin.

> I had the honour of two of your Lordships the last week, since which I have been till now out of the road of all Posts, being employed to find Horses in the Country for drawing the cannon from Liége to Limburgh, those whose business it properly was having so wholly neglected it that there wanted above a thousand, which with much ado I have got att last and sent away to Liége from whence all the Cannon and Mortars left behind will be brought this night to Limburgh and in eight or ten days wee shall be masters of that place.

On a lighter note Cadogan in a post-script writes that 'Your Lordship in your letter speaks of your old mistress in Ireland, but I had much rather have news of some of the new ones you make att Berlin.'[2] An understandable sentiment after a long and demanding campaigning season. The Allied troops improved upon Cadogan's forecast and on the 26th September Limburgh duly fell; shortly thereafter both sides began to take up their winter quarters. It had been a satisfactory year for the Allies with the security of the United Provinces finally assured.

In December Cadogan took a short leave in London, returning to Marlborough's headquarters at the Hague early in 1704. In addition to his usual winter problems of forage and quartering he also had much on his mind a certain Miss Margaretha Munter, a 28-year-old Dutch heiress and daughter of a noble family from Amsterdam. At 31 it was time for the Quartermaster-General, with his professional career in the ascendant, to think of matrimony.

[34]

Countess Cadogan
(née Margaretha Munter)

Prince Eugène

Before that, however, there were other matters to attend to and at the beginning of March Cadogan set sail again for England carrying papers for the Duke of Marlborough. During the North Sea crossing the paquet boat that carried Cadogan was attacked by a privateer out from Dunkirk and in the ensuing fight, when it looked as though things would go badly for him, Cadogan threw his papers overboard to avoid the possibility of their falling into French hands. The fore top mast and the main mast were shot through and all appeared lost. At the critical moment however, when the English crew were about to strike their colours, a brisk wind sprang up and the paquet boat was able to claw its way out of trouble, arriving at Harwich on the 7th March. Colonel Cadogan had returned to the Hague by the 23rd

March when the banns of his forthcoming marriage to Margaretha were published. The marriage took place eighteen days later at the Walloon Church there.

The newly-weds were able to pass their honeymoon in comparative peace as it was not until the beginning of May that the English army emerged from their winter quarters, to be reviewed by Marlborough on the 11th of the month at Maastricht, twenty miles north-west of Aix-la-Chapelle. Seven days later the army had moved west to Bedburg which lay fifteen miles from Cologne and the banks of the Rhine. The major issue facing the Allies at this time was the Franco-Bavarian threat to Vienna, the capital of the Holy Roman Empire and the weak link of the Grand Alliance as its loss would almost certainly mean the collapse of the Allied structure. Marlborough's plan therefore was to bring the Franco-Bavarian army to battle so as to remove the pressure from Vienna. This necessitated a forced march by the Allied army, at this stage comprising 21,000 men, from Bedburg which they left on the 19th May to Launsheim close to Ulm on the River Danube where they arrived on the 22nd June. The Duke's army had covered a distance of more than 250 miles in a little over five weeks, a major military feat of endurance and organisation. Little wonder that Prince Eugène of Savoy, on inspecting part of Marlborough's cavalry on the 11th June, had declared, 'My Lord, I never saw better horses, better clothes, finer belts and accoutrements, but money which you don't want in England, will buy fine clothes and fine horses, but it can't buy that lively air I see in every one of these troopers faces.'[3] A fine compliment not only for the Duke but also for Colonel Cadogan's organisational abilities which were clearly demonstrated again on the march to Launsheim. Earlier, on the 30th May Cadogan had written to Lord Raby 'This march has hardly left me time to eat or sleep . . .'. A diarist of the day recorded that 'Surely never was such a march carried on with more order and regularity and with less fatigue to man and horse.'[4]

At Launsheim Marlborough's Allied army had swelled to 40,000 men and by this time he had linked up with his Allied commanders, Prince Eugène and the Margrave of Baden. Together they commanded a force of 110,000 men. After a council-of-war Prince Eugène returned eastwards with 28,000 men to Stollhofen to maintain a watch on the French army there while the Duke and the Margrave marched further west arriving at the fortress of Donauworth on the 2nd July. Here they surprised the local Bavarian commander and his garrison of 10,000 men and a bloody battle followed for the control of the Schellenberg Heights which were the key to victory. Not surprisingly the garrison troops were soon overborne although the Allies gain was costly; they lost 1342 men killed and 3699 wounded. The French and Bavarian forces suffered a loss of 5000 men. Colonel Cadogan at the head of his regiment greatly distinguished himself in the thick of the fighting; his horse was shot from under him, he had several shots through his clothes and he was wounded in the thigh.

Although the victory at Donauworth was good for morale the Allies had yet to meet the main Franco-Bavarian army which for the time being was pursuing a policy of masterly inactivity. The Allies had therefore to content themselves with a successful siege of Rain during the period 9-16th July at the same time as ravaging the Bavarian

THE GLORIOUS BATTLE
of BLENHEIM
August the 13 1704

countryside and destroying close on four hundred villages. At last, however, on the 13th August a major battle was joined at the village of Blenheim fifteen miles east of Donauworth. An Allied force of 52,000 men led by Marlborough and Eugène faced 56,000 French and Bavarians. The fighting raged all day and by evening the enemy were well and truly routed, losing 20,000 men killed and wounded, with a further 14,000 taken prisoner. In all close on two-thirds of the enemy army had been destroyed. The Allies sustained some 3000 killed and 10,000 wounded. Blenheim was an undoubted victory for the Allies; Vienna and the Grand Alliance were saved. Colonel Cadogan's 'valour greatly contributed to the success of the cavalry'[5] and accordingly on the 25th August 1704 he was promoted brigadier-general. One historian has written that the 'success of the Blenheim campaign was largely due [to Cadogan's] skilful arrangements as Quartermaster-General'.[6]

The Allies followed up their advantage, taking Ulm and Ingolstadt and with them the whole of Bavaria. Soon afterwards the Allied army separated to take up winter quarters and General Cadogan returned to the Hague. The French for the time being had been replaced by the English as military masters of Europe. For Cadogan the year had been a very satisfactory one; he had married into a wealthy family of standing, escaped near capture and death and been promoted to general rank. In addition his name was included in the distribution list of the Queen's bounty for Blenheim in the sums of £90 as Brigadier-General, £60 as Quartermaster-General and £123 as Colonel of a regiment of horse and Captain of a troop therein.[7]

The following year of 1705 was generally a disappointing one for the Allies, due in the main to the intransigence of the Dutch and the only major action fought was the breaching of the Lines of Brabant on the 17/18th July at Elixhem forty miles south-east of Brussels. The enemy, on this occasion comprising Spanish and Bavarian horse and Bavarian foot, were thoroughly beaten. Cadogan's Horse 'won great distinction'[8] in driving off the field the famous Bavarian horse-grenadier guards and capturing four of their standards. According to popular accounts the charge was lead in person by Cadogan. Perhaps, however, the most auspicious event of the year for Cadogan was his election at Marlborough's nomination as Member of Parliament for

Woodstock in the May General Election, when the Whigs secured a majority in the Commons. It would be some time before he addressed Parliament but when he eventually did so it was in support of Whig policy.

The Duke of Marlborough's favourite scheme for 1706 was a return to the Moselle-Saar region, but Dutch timidity forced him to undertake a further campaign in the Spanish Netherlands. He took the field on the 13th May therefore and began to assemble the Allied troops at Tongres situated on the River Jaar, fifteen miles north-west of Liége, convinced that after the rout at Blenheim the enemy would not fight unless compelled to do so. The French, however, were determined to avenge the events of the previous year and accordingly an army under Marshal Villeroi, comprising 74 battalions and 128 squadrons, was at that moment heading south bent on confrontation. The news came as a welcome surprise to the Allies who by now had mustered a similar number of battalions and 122 squadrons. (According to contemporary records, a battalion in theory would number 1000 men. In practice, the number could be less. A squadron was 'a Body of Horse, the number not fixt, but from one hundred to two hundred Men'. A regiment would consist of two battalions.)[9] The two armies closed at a faster pace than either side realised and the 22nd May found them only twenty miles or so apart, the Allies at Corswaren and the French, unbeknown to the Allies, close to the village of Ramillies. In the early hours of the morning of the 23rd May Cadogan was ordered by his commander to ride ahead through dense fog with six hundred horse to reconnoitre for the next camp and shortly afterwards the main army followed in three large columns, still without knowledge of the enemy's position. At eight o'clock that same morning Cadogan had just passed Merdorp when he came into contact with a detachment of French hussars. The fog then cleared to reveal to Cadogan the French army massing on the horizon and he immediately sent an aide to gallop the news back to Marlborough who, within two hours, had joined his Quartermaster-General.

The guns opened fire close to one o'clock in the afternoon. The battle raged to and fro, but by six o'clock in the evening Marlborough was able to order the general attack. The French army was shattered and in the ensuing melee the Allies captured fifty cannon and eighty standards and colours. Cadogan had been in the thick of the action and was fortunate not to be included in the Allies' 3500 casualties. The French had sustained some 13,000 dead and wounded. After Ramillies the Allies swept all before them

The Battle of Ramillies

and on the 25th May they occupied Louvain, three days later taking Brussels, the capital of the Spanish Netherlands. Meanwhile Cadogan had been sent with a body of horse and foot to occupy Ghent and to call upon the City of Antwerp to surrender, missions which were speedily accomplished. The Antwerp garrison, comprising twelve French and Spanish regiments, were allowed to march out and the keys of the city were handed to Cadogan, their first surrender since they were given up to the Duke of Parma after a twelve-month siege two hundred years before. In recognition of his outstanding service, Cadogan was promoted to the rank of major general as from the 1st June 1706.

By the 5th August, after a successful siege of Ostend, the Allies had moved south-east and laid siege to the French garrison town of Menin. It was here that the incident of Marlborough's glove took place. The Duke had ridden out with Cadogan and his staff to reconnoitre the enemy's position at close quarters when he dropped his glove. In the normal course of events this would have been retrieved by one of the Duke's equerries, but on this occasion he asked Cadogan to pick it up and of course the Quartermaster-General complied instantly. Returned to camp, the Duke reminded Cadogan of the occurrence, adding that he wished a battery of guns to be positioned on the spot. Cadogan replied that he had already given the order and, on Marlborough expressing surprise, Cadogan explained that he knew his commander to be too much a gentleman to make such a request without good hidden reason and he had guessed what it was. This is a fine example of the degree of understanding that had evolved between the two men. Menin capitulated on the 21st August.

[42]

The supply of the army was among Cadogan's many duties and on the 16th August, while making a forage near Tournai twenty miles south-east of Menin in the combined capacities of a cavalry commander and Quartermaster-General, he was captured by the enemy. Cadogan's friend Lord Raby, now a major-general himself and Ambassador extraordinary to Berlin, who was accompanying him as a volunteer narrowly escaped and this prompted Cadogan to write to Raby on the following day:

I received with all the pleasure imaginable the honour of Your Lordship's obliging letter. I assure your Lordship the greatest pain I had when I was taken, was my apprehension for Your Lordship's safety, which I was not assured till my Trumpet came in the evening. I was thrust by the crowd I endeavoured to stop, into a ditch on the right of the way we passed, with great difficulty I got out of it and with greater good fortune escaped falling into the Hussars' hands who first came up with me. [Cadogan goes on to say that he eventually fell] to the share of the French Carabiniers who followed their Hussars and Dragoons from whom wee met with quarters and civility baring their taking my watch and money. My Lord Duke has been so extremely kind as to propose exchanging the Marquis de Croissy for me so I hope my prison will not be of very long consequence.[10]

The Duke did not know at the outset whether his indispens-able right-hand man was taken prisoner or killed and in a state of some perturbation he had immediately written a note from his camp at Helchin to the French commandant at Tournai: 'Monsieur le Quartier-Maitre General Cadogan qui est sorti ce matin avec nos fourrageurs n'etant pas encore de retour et ayant appris qu'il pourrait bien etre pris par quelques troupes de votre garrison, j'envoire ce Trompette pour vous prier d'avoir la bonté de m'en informer, et de l'état ou il se trouve. Je vous en aurai beaucoup d'obligation, etant avec une veritable passion.' In the chivalrous manner of the age, the commandant replied that Cadogan was indeed both alive and well and it was eventually agreed to exchange him not for the Marquis de Croissy as Cadogan thought would be the case but for Lieutenant-General Pallavicini who had been in Allied hands since Ramillies. Thus Cadogan returned to join Marlborough at Helchin.

A month later on the 26th September Cadogan's first child, a daughter, was baptised Sarah at St Jacobskerk at the Hague. It seems unlikely that he would have been able to attend this happy event as the Allies were very much pre-occupied with the siege of Ath, twenty miles to the east of Tournai, which was not resolved until the 2nd October. The taking of Ath proved to be the last Allied conquest of 1706 and, following a review of the army by Marlborough on the 25th October, the troops dispersed into their winter quarters. That year's campaign had been very successful for the Grand Alliance and the Allies had every reason to feel optimism about the coming twelve months.

In addition to his winter quartering duties for the English army, Cadogan had also been engaged in the politically sensitive matter of finding suitable winter quarters for the Allied troops, including the Prussians. His letter to Lord Raby dated the 12th November and addressed from the Hague throws an interesting light upon the Quartermaster-General's perquisites of office.

The affair of the winter quarters for the Troops of Prussia is very near settled. We shall give half the bread and the agio [charge for changing one currency into another] in these places where the German money is not currant and agree with the Country to furnish all the forrage for which the Queen and the States will be answerable. I believe I have been very serviceable to the Prussian Troops in the whole course of this affair, the first project of which and to which I have not a little assisted to give the finishing stroke since my being hence. This I suppose procured me the Order of Generosity [from the King of Prussia] which was a greater surprise to me than to anybody else . . . My Lord Duke has writt to the Queen for leave for me to wear it. I am told there is a thousand Ducats designed for me to buye a Jewel as soon as the affair of the winter quarters is fully regulated. This as your Lordship rightly judges will make the Order more welcome, but I cannot at the same time help telling your Lordship that there is hardly any of the little Princes in Germany who have troops here, that have not acknowledged much more considerably the services I have done them in the business of the winter quarters.[11]

During the following month of December Cadogan received further confirmation of his favourable standing both with Marlborough and Queen Anne when he was appointed Lieutenant of the Tower of London, an ancient office dating from 1189. Although the position had become increasingly honorary it carried pay at the rate of £1.13s.4¼d a day and while Cadogan would not have had much time to devote to Tower affairs it gave him easy access to the greatest centre of armament in Britain. Certainly in his role as Quartermaster-General he would have interested himself in the weapon trials and production which were supervised by the Office of Ordnance based in the Tower of London. Perhaps it was this interest which brought about his introduction of enfilade or defensive fire into the artillery manual.

Major-General Cadogan had every reason to share the Allies' mood of optimism and to look forward to the coming year.

[45]

CHAPTER V

The War of
the Spanish Succession
– The Middle Years

During the winter months Cadogan spent some time in England, searching for an estate to use as a home in his adopted country. His choice settled upon the Manor of Oakley in Buckinghamshire, which comprised the manor house and some 373 acres of mainly pasture land located twelve miles north-east of Oxford. The previous Lord of this ancient manor, dating back to the eleventh century, was one James Tyrell and the price paid by Cadogan at completion in March 1707 was £9450.[1] The red-brick house with stone dressings was built in 1666 and, besides being quite modern, it had for Cadogan the additional advantage of being only twenty miles from Woodstock, his parliamentary constituency and the site Marlborough had chosen for the construction of his future home at Blenheim Palace. The accommodation provided by the manor house was quite modest and comprised on the ground floor a small entrance hall, a drawing room twenty feet square, a kitchen about fifteen feet square and two long rooms running the length of the house about nine feet wide which appear to

Manor House, Oakley

have been used for food storage. The first floor which led to an attic store offered two bedrooms similar in size to the main rooms on the ground floor together with a third room measuring twelve feet by nine feet. It seems likely that Cadogan had plans to enlarge the house or perhaps, in the light of subsequent events, he viewed the purchase only as an interim step to something on a grander scale. Oakley House remains to this day, albeit with the interior re-arranged.

Cadogan returned to the Hague at the end of March and discovered that, in the words of Sir Winston Churchill, 'the Grand Alliance was once again found incapable of enduring success'.[2] One of the problems that had arisen was the governance of the recently conquered Flemish-speaking provinces of the Spanish Netherlands, taken by the Allies after Ramillies. There the Dutch were at odds with the Austrians over the garrisoning of those towns which the

[47]

Dutch felt were vital to their particular interest insofar as the setting up of a fortress barrier against the French was concerned. The dispute revolved around the matter of Regency and in the end a compromise was reached whereby the area in dispute was ruled by a Flemish Council of State on behalf of King Charles VI of Austria under the joint-Regency of England and Holland. England was represented by Marlborough who was later aided by Cadogan. The device worked well but the issue of the Dutch barrier was to remain a bone of contention between the Allies for the duration of the war. As further events unfolded the Allies' earlier optimism proved to be quite unfounded and it became increasingly clear that the French war machine was far from a spent force. The Duc d'Orléans had a major success at Almanza in Spain on the 25th April while Marshal Villars gained a surprise victory over the Imperial forces at Stollhofen towards the end of May, putting the Danube once again under threat. In the following months the Allies were unsuccessful in bringing the French to battle in Flanders while in August Prince Eugène was thwarted in his attempt on Toulon in the south of France. By mid-September the Allies were relieved to be able to withdraw once again into their winter quarters.

Cadogan in his personal matters had fared rather better than the Allies and on the 16th June from his camp at Meldert he was able to write to Lord Raby, promoted this year to the rank of lieutenant-general, that

I received an account from Holland that the wine Your Lordship was pleased to send me was come to the Hague for which you will give me leave to return you a thousand thanks. Mon'er Cromkaw [the Prussian representative at the Hague] brought me a cross with a Diamond [presumably the King of Prussia's 'Order of Generosity'] of about three score or four score pounds value at the utmost. I accepted it with the same deference and respect as if it had been worth five hundred.[3]

Whether Cadogan received his one thousand ducats is not recorded.

During October Cadogan accompanied Marlborough on a visit to the Rhine and on his return he found waiting for him a letter from James Brydges in London, the Queen's Paymaster-General of the Forces abroad and a contemporary of Cadogan at Westminster School. 'This is chiefly to congratulate you upon two pieces of good news that the town is full of, one is that you have won six thousand Pistoles at play, the other is that you are to retire at the Hague in the room of Mr. Stepney . . .' The first piece of news had presumably not reached Cadogan's friend Lord Raby who subsequently wrote to him on the 1st November scolding him for succumbing to his weakness for gambling and losing money. 'I thought you had shook of that passion', he told Cadogan. The second piece of news Brydges referred to is covered by an eventual entry in the Queen's Warrant Book dated the 28th November 1707 which reads 'Privy Seal dated at our Palace of Westminster for £500 to Major-General William Cadogan for his equipage and £5 a day as Ordinary, as Envoy Extraordinary to the States-General and as Plenipotentiary in negotiations we are entered into in concert with other Princes and States for what relates to the common interest, the said Ordinary to commence from the 1st November instant.' Cadogan's new appointment took him first to the Hague where he signed Treaties made for the Prussian quarters and forage as well as the bargains made for the forage to be sent to the

Hanoverian and the Danish troops fighting with the Allies. He travelled then to the 'open city' of Brussels where many problems awaited his attention including the exchange of prisoners with the French and negotiating for loans, one of which was for 400,000 Guilders on the 'Dutys and Customs of Ostend'. Cadogan wrote from Brussels on the 19th January 1708 to Lord Raby,

> I assure your Lordship that nothing like a hint about peace passed at our conference for the exchange of prisoners, so far from it, the French talked in their old insolent style, and threatened eternal war and destruction rather than give up any part of the Spanish Monarchy. Wee could not agree . . . the business of the Exchange [of prisoners], they insisting on an entire releasement of all their prisoners General Officers included, by which they would have got forty General Officers for five, and of others in a less character three for one.' [Cadogan concludes the letter to his friend] I will give you in a few words the description of Brussels. Count Corneille is the Principal Trickster and [Count] Oxenstiern [a Dutch general] the Top Wit. My Lord Aylesbury a shining Beau, and his Lady a celebrated Tost, not a woman but puts on as much red as my Lady Falkland, and is as coquette as our former friend my Lady S——n. They play deep and pay ill, and in short there is a tolerable deal of scandal but no f——ng. Tho to doe the women Justice tis not their fault.[4]

Cadogan returned to the Hague at the end of the month where the Allies were discussing the strategy to be adopted for the coming campaign.

The French meanwhile were planning to capitalise upon the unpopularity in Scotland of the Act of Union passed by Parliament in 1706 which signalled the legislative union of Scotland with England as from the 1st of May 1707. They intended to invade the highlands of what was now Great Britain in the hope of fomenting a civil war between the supporters of Queen Anne and those of James the 'Pretender', son of the late King James II, now living in France. The French hope was that any civil commotion would cause the English to withdraw at least some of their troops from mainland Europe and so make the French task there that much easier. The invasion was planned for the month of March and the 20-year-old Pretender was to accompany a force of 6000 men with an escort of 5 men-of-war and 15 privateers. Word of the French design reached London and caused Marlborough to send a despatch to Cadogan.

Her Majesty has thought fit you forthwith repair to Flanders and by all means inform yourself of the enemy's designs, giving notice of what you learn by every opportunity, and if you find it requisite by frequent expresses both by Ostend and the Brill [Dutch port]. Her Majesty does likewise think fit in case there be any good grounds to believe the enemy have formed a design of landing in these parts or in North Britain, that there be a proportional number of her Foot forces not only kept in readiness to embark immediately, but does further recommend it your care if the enemy should embark with an intention of landing in Great Britain before you have any other order from hence, that then you put her troops on shipboard with all possible speed either at Ostend or in Zealand . . .

Cadogan went immediately to Ostend and proceeded to gather intelligence from the Allies' agents at Mons and Lille which he duly relayed to Marlborough. This enabled counter-measures to be put in hand, one of them being that Admiral Byng sailed with a force of eighteen English and Dutch men-of-war to blockade the enemy port of Dunkirk. Local militias were put into a state of readiness and ten regiments of foot serving in Flanders were sent to Ostend under Cadogan and Brigadier Sabine, where they embarked on the 15th March, sailing two days later in a convoy of ten warships. The weather was stormy causing the blockading squadron to break formation and this enabled the French to put out from Dunkirk on the 17th March, arriving at the Firth of Forth on the 19th March. Their reception by the native Scots was not encouraging and this, together with the close presence of Admiral Byng's fleet in hot pursuit, caused them to call a halt to the adventure. Cadogan and his men arrived back at the Hague on the 12th April, at which time Marlborough and Prince Eugène were on the point of concluding their conference with the Dutch States-General.

Marlborough's plan for 1708 was to divide the Allied forces in the Netherlands and Germany into three armies, the largest of which, comprising 100 battalions and 150 squadrons, he would retain under his personal command in Flanders. The second army was to form on the Moselle under Prince Eugène while the third army was to operate on the Upper Rhine under George, Elector of Hanover, the future King George I of England. There were the usual recruiting delays and it was not until the 21st May that Marlborough's army, approaching 90,000 in strength, assembled at Anderlecht near Brussels. The Allied aim was, as in the previous year, to bring the French to battle in the hope of clearing a way through to the French heartland. The French, meanwhile, despite severe domestic economic problems were able to field five armies the largest of which amounted to 131 battalions and 216 squadrons under the joint command of the King's grandson the 26-year-old Duc de Bourgogne and the older Marshal Louis-Joseph, Duc de Vendôme. This army was under orders to campaign in Flanders with the aim of drawing Marlborough's army away from the French borders. On the 26th May the French army crossed the River Haine and moved towards Hal, camping at Soignies, whereupon the Allied army proceeded to take up a position south of Hal. Neither side wished at this juncture to bring the other to battle, the French because of differences between the joint commanders and the British because Marlborough was waiting for Prince Eugène and his army to join him so as to gain closer parity with the enemy. A period of inactivity followed and this was not broken until the first week in July when French forces stole a march on Marlborough and took the cities of Bruges and Ghent, in so doing recapturing much of Spanish Flanders, to the dismay of the Allies.

The bulk of Bourgogne's army had now crossed over the River Dender to the north of Ath, so placing itself between the Allied army and Ostend, the nearest point of communication with England. Marlborough's army in an effort to rectify the position caught up with the tail of the French army south of Ninove but the French escaped battle by resorting to a *ruse de guerre*. According to one Sergeant Millner, the French army 'falsified and flourished its colours in the scrub in our front, as if all their army had been there a-posting to give our army battle'.[5] Meantime of course the main body of the enemy had passed on its way. Marlborough at this time was suffering from one of his occasional bouts of migraine and one historian has written that 'Cadogan was away visiting Eugène – which perhaps accounts for the success of this trick'.[6] The incident may underline the importance of Cadogan's presence to the success of the Allied cause. The vital question now was whether the French could consolidate their control of the central Scheldt by taking Oudenarde before the Allies could move in reinforcements. At this point the Allies were assisted by some further disagreement in the French joint command which resulted in an enemy decision only to blockade Oudenarde and to march on the 9th July towards nearby Lessines. This move enabled the Allies to reinforce Oudenarde and they were also able to make preparations to secure the crossing points on the River Dender before the French arrival, by which time Prince Eugène had joined up with Marlborough.

On the afternoon of the 9th July, as part of the Allied initiative Cadogan set off from Herfelingen at the head of an advance guard of eight battalions and eight squadrons. The main army followed in the early hours of the morning of the 10th July and throughout that day both the Allied and the French armies were approaching Lessines from opposite directions. Cadogan was first in the town and this resulted in the French veering away northwards to Gavre on the east bank of the Scheldt where they encamped that night. Marlborough's army came to rest on the west bank of the River Dender south-east of Oudenarde. Only fifteen short miles now separated the two armies and a clash seemed inevitable. Marlborough decided to attempt to cross the River Scheldt before the French and to reach Oudenarde as quickly as possible. This necessitated the building of pontoon bridges and accordingly at one o'clock in the morning of the 11th July Cadogan set out along the Oudenarde road with sixteen battalions of British infantry, eight squadrons of Hanoverian dragoons commanded by the Elector's son George, the future King George II of England, and thirty-two regimental guns. He also had

The PASSAGE
of the
Scheld.
1708.

under his command the whole of the pontoon train and a detachment of pioneers. Cadogan had orders to build five pontoon bridges over the Scheldt just north of Oudenarde and, this task accomplished, to establish a bridgehead.

On reaching the river Cadogan sighted the French encampment six miles away on the heights of Gavre. He had won the race to the river and he now proceeded to build the required bridges. This was a demanding job as each pontoon or flat-bottomed boat was about seventeen feet long and made of wood strengthened with copper plates. These were launched into the water, anchored at set intervals and then linked by heavy beams with a plank roadway laid atop. Notwithstanding the difficulties of the situation the bridges were completed and the first battalions across the river by mid-day. The French in the meantime did not begin their crossing up river until 10 a.m. Battle was joined there three hours later and the scene was set for an epic struggle. The Allied army comprised, on the day, 85 battalions and 150 squadrons as against a French strength of 90 battalions and 170 squadrons: in terms of actual troops, 80,000 as against 90,000. The Allies eventually triumphed due to 'French confusions'[7] with a loss of 825 killed and 2150 wounded. The French losses were of a similar order although in addition some 7000 of their men, including 700 officers, were taken prisoner. Cadogan was in the van of the battle and absorbed sufficient of the enemy's initial thrust to enable Marlborough to bring his main army into the fray. Cadogan's younger brother Charles, an officer in Cadogan's Horse, also fought at Oudenarde.

The victory at Oudenarde regained the initiative for the Allies who now had to decide how best to consolidate their

Charles Cadogan

advantage. The decision taken was to march south-west to Lille, the capital of French Flanders, 'next to Paris . . . reckon'd the chief place of His Most Christian Majesty's dominions'.[8] The capture of Lille would disrupt French trade and provide an excellent base for the next campaign; it would also serve further to depress French morale. Towards the end of July Cadogan wrote to Brydges,

Wee are still in our camp at Werwick in order to besiege Lille as soon as our heavy cannon comes up which I hope will be by the 6th of next month n.s. at the farthest. You may easily imagine the trouble and difficulties of bringing it by land from Brussels to Lille which is the reason of our present inaction, tho' in the mean while we ravage Artois in Picardy [northern France], and could entirely burn and destroy these two provinces but the Dutch choose rather to make them contribute . . . Wee still have enough of the summer to take Lisle [Lille] and Tournay, the scene of the Warr will then be removed into France as has so long

[57]

been wish'd for . . . I shall come up with the convoy from Brussels, his Grace having charged me with the care of that convoy . . .

The convoy to which Cadogan referred was the 'Great Convoy' which included 80 siege pieces and 20 siege mortars each pulled by 20 and 16 horses respectively and 3000 munition waggons each drawn by 4 horses. The convoy stretched for thirty miles and it required all of Cadogan's considerable administrative skills to ensure that it reached Lille where the siege began on the 13th August. This had been a testing time not only for Cadogan but also for Marlborough who wrote to his Quartermaster-General on the 3rd August: 'For Gods sake be sure you do not risk the cannon'.[9] The loss of the convoy would clearly have meant the end of the Allies' hopes to take Lille. According to an eminent Dutch historian, 'Cadogan again showed himself to be a staff officer of great ability.'

The French made no move towards relieving Lille and instead they adopted the strategy of endeavouring to cut the Allies' lines of supply. At this point Marlborough and Cadogan seemed inclined to abandon the siege but Prince Eugène who was actually undertaking the operation, mostly with Dutch and Imperial troops, remained of the view that it should continue, and so it did. Cadogan now in camp at Helchin, fifteen miles north-east of Lille, wrote to Brydges

Lille is now besieged . . . Prince Eugene commands att the siege and his army is made up by a detachment from ours to 100 squadrons and 56 battalions . . . My Lord Duke is encamped here with the army of observation which consists of 22 battalions and 143 squadrons. The resolution is to attack Monsieur Vendome the minute he comes from behind the canal of Gent [Ghent]. We have a garrison of 10 battalion and

7 squadrons att Brussels, Antwerp, Ostend and Dutch Flanders and are more than sufficiently provided so that in the present situation of affairs, our game seems to be as sure as anything in war can be.

By the 23rd September the French in their war of supply had taken every crossing point over the River Scheldt, thus isolating the siege force from its supply bases. If the siege was to continue it was vital for the Allies to find an alternative supply route and accordingly a large convoy of 700 wagons was assembled at the Allied-held port of Ostend, from where it departed on the 27th September with an escort of twelve battalions and fifteen hundred horse. Two days earlier an Allied force of 6000 infantrymen under the command of Major-General Webb had decamped from Lannoy to afford greater protection for the convoy. On the 28th September it met with a mixed French force of some 18,000 infantrymen and cavalry under Count de la Motte at Wynendael, fifteen miles south-east of Ostend. General Webb's men, much outnumbered by the enemy, fought well and were gaining the upper hand when Cadogan arrived with a column of cavalry. This reinforcement finally turned the tables and the enemy withdrew. Marlborough later wrote to Lord Godolphin, the Queen's Lord Treasurer, 'Webb and Cadogan have on this occasion, as they always will do, behaved themselves extremely well. The success of this vigorous action is, in a great measure, due to them. If they had not succeeded and our convoy had been lost the consequences must have been the raising of the siege next day.'[10] As it was, the convoy reached its destination on the 29th September with enough supplies to sustain the siege for a further two weeks. Many more supply trains were subsequently necessary and later the Allies' task was made

The Battle of Wynendael

doubly difficult by the French flooding the polders in western Flanders. Cadogan displayed great ingenuity in conveying munitions and rations, first in low flat-bottomed boats from Ostend to Lessingues, from where they were transferred onto waggons with over-sized wheels. Marlborough paid this tribute to his premier aide: 'In this difficult task, Cadogan distinguished himself, as he did on every occasion, which required extraordinary diligence and activity, and convoys were brought in safety in spite of hostile batteries and incessant attacks of armed gallies.'

The city of Lille finally surrendered on the 25th October although the citadel held out until the 9th December. The Allied victory had been achieved at a cost of 15,000 casualties. The campaign continued unusually late in 1708 and it was not until the 30th December that Ghent was retaken, followed by the surrender of Bruges the following day. 'When Major-General Cadogan, at the head of a strong detachment approached the town [of Ghent] the inhabitants hastened to welcome the Allied troops, hardly waiting the French retreat.' After a good start to the year the French had suffered badly from the military viewpoint and low morale in the army was exacerbated by famine at home and civilian unrest. Cadogan along with others would have considered the portents favourable for peace after seven long years of war.

CHAPTER VI

The War of
the Spanish Succession
– Closing Years
and a New Commander

The new year of 1709 opened well for Cadogan and on the 1st January he was promoted to the rank of lieutenant-general. He was now 36 years old. The winter was exceptionally bitter and men and horses froze to death. Cadogan had the unenviable task of travelling frequently in this extreme weather between the Hague and Brussels, a journey of a hundred miles, and from the Hague on the 22nd February he wrote to Lord Raby,

The several turns I have made between this place and Brussells since the ending of the campaign, and my being frequently obliged to goe to Leuse, when the conference is held about the exchange of prisoners, has made me lead as rambling a life the winter as I did in the summer. . . His Grace has The Enemy's designs, but put us in a condition of prosecuting effectually the advantages of the last campaign, of which wee ought to reap the benefit this, since by the having Lille we have broken thro' the French barrier in its strongest part. All the rumours and storys of peace, and of French agents being here are absolutely false and groundless and tho' I believe this Republick heartily tired of the war, yet I am persuaded they will hearken to no other peace than the entire restitution of the Spanish Monarchy which the French think their affairs are not in so ill a position as to oblige them to consent to.

Economic and allied supply problems did, however, force the French king to send President Rouille to the Hague during the following month to seek peace proposals from the States-General. These negotiations in the end, to the Allie's surprise, came to nought and preparations then had to be quickly advanced for a further campaign.

By mid-June the Allies had brought together an army, concentrated at Ghent, of 152 battalions and 245 squadrons with reinforcements expected from the smaller European powers now eager to share the spoils of conquest. It seemed quite clear that if victory was to be achieved it would happen on French soil. The French army, centred on Douai, with a strength on paper of 150 battalions and 220 squadrons, was to be commanded this season by Marshal Villars. The Allied generals met in council and it was agreed that before a campaign objective could be decided upon it would be necessary to undertake a full reconnaissance of French positions on either side of the River Deule. Two men volunteered for the mission; one was General Dopf and the other was Cadogan, only recently recovered from an 'indisposition'. Dopf undertook his quest for intelligence in the traditional manner with a cavalry escort; Cadogan on the other hand went off alone disguised as a peasant to enable him to penetrate more deeply into enemy territory. Cadogan by now both spoke and wrote French fluently and the information that he gathered persuaded the Allied high command that a frontal assault on the French lines would be inadvisable, so they eventually decided to invest Tournai, situated some fifteen miles south-east of Lille.

The Siege of Tournai

Tournai was taken on the 5th September but the victory
was hard-won with the Allies sustaining over 5000 casualties. To maintain pressure on the enemy Marlborough then

immediately marched his men south-east to invest Mons, which offered the opportunity of out-flanking the French lines. The manoeuvre caused Louis to send an urgent message to Villars that 'should Mons follow on the fate of Tournai, our case is undone; you are by every means in your power to relieve the garrison; the cost is not to be considered; the salvation of France is at stake'.[1] So exhorted, Villars moved his army from its defensive position at Douai and marched on Mons to be met by the Allied army on the 11th September at Malplaquet, ten miles south-west of the beleaguered city. There took place what has been described as 'the most desperate and bloody attack and battle that had been fought in the memory of men'.[2] The confederate army was victorious and Cadogan is recorded as having played 'a conspicuous part'[3] in the battle, again fighting alongside his brother Charles. The cost to the Allies was dear, having lost near 25,000 men killed and wounded. Among those killed were the 'Top Wit' General Oxenstiern of whom Cadogan had written to Lord Raby in 1708 and Cadogan's brother-in-law Brigadier-General Sir Thomas Prendergast, married to his sister Penelope, who was 'mortally wounded while bravely leading his regiment to the assault of the French troops entrenched in the wood of Blaregnies'.[4] Cadogan wrote after this terrible battle that 'Our loss is very considerable, but the enemy's infinitely more.' Marlborough sent him under a flag of truce to meet the Duc de Luxembourg at Bavai to make arrangements for the evacuation of the enemy wounded.

As the French retreated the Allies intensified the siege of Mons and Cadogan was despatched thither with a corps of infantry, 200 guns and 50 mortars. 'He constantly went into

The Battle of Malplaquet

the trenches to encourage his men, and on one occasion his aide-de-camp was killed at his side and he himself was severely wounded in the neck.'[5] On the 26th September Marlborough wrote to his wife Sarah:

After a great deal of trouble we have at last gott some part of our artillerie from Bruxelles so that we open'd last night the trenches, where poor Cadogan was wound'd in the neck. I hope he will do well, but til he recovers it will oblige me to do many things, by which I shall have but little rest. I was with him this morning when they drest his wound. As he is very fatt there greatest aprehension is growing feaverish. We must have patience for two or three dressings before the surjeans can give their judgement. I hope in God he will do well, for I can intierly depend upon him.[6]

Marlborough with Cadogan (on the grey horse) and other members of his staff

When news of Cadogan's wound reached London, Brydges wrote to him:

Wee were very much surpriz'd at the occasion of it, and hoped your other employments and business had so much taken up your time as to have prevented our danger of losing a person so valuable to his country on such sort of service, but last post brought the wellcome news of your being in a fair way of recovery, at which I heartily rejoice, and hope it will prove a warning to you how you expose yourself on such like occasions again . . .

Cadogan recovered and the following month he returned to Brussels. Mons capitulated on the 20th October and eight days later the army began to break up again for winter quarters. On the 2nd December Cadogan wrote to Marlborough that 'Great numbers of deserters come in daily.

[67]

They are half starved and quite naked, and give such an account of the misery the French troops are in, as could not be believed were it not confirmed by the reports and letters from all their garrison towns on the frontier.'[7] Cheering news indeed for the Captain-General. In England the portents were less promising for Marlborough; although the Whig Ministry secured him a vote of thanks from Parliament for his services at Malplaquet, his enemies in the Tory ranks accused him of obtaining corrupt financial gains and of failing to secure peace. Thus the seeds were sown for Marlborough's fall from grace.

The French made further overtures for peace early in 1710 and talks took place with the Allies at Gertruidenburg, forty miles south-east of the Hague, in March. As usual the question of Spain proved the stumbling-block. Various propositions were put forward by both sides including the Allies' suggestion of a separate peace being concluded with France leaving aside the Spanish question, but all to no avail and the talks eventually came to an inconclusive end in July. Once again Allied disunity was in evidence and, 'As the opportunities for a brilliant and decisive campaign were opening to the Allies, their ability to take advantage of them was dwindling.'[8] The Allied campaign opened with an investment of Douai about which Cadogan wrote to the Earl of Sunderland, Marlborough's son-in-law,

After taking this place there is nothing to stop our piercing into France with this great and victorious army, but the town of Arras which is weak in itself can be no ways defended but by the enemy's giving a battel which, considering the present situation of things, the disadvantages they must venture on it, and the fatal consequences which will attend the loss of it, 'tis not to be imagined they will hasard.

Cadogan was right for the French king was firm in his resolve that any major battle this season was to be avoided at all costs. After stiff resistance, Douai fell to the Allies on the 27th June at a cost of 8000 casualties, yet more ammunition for the ever-mounting body of critics at home who thought that the time had come for a negotiated peace. The Allies went on to successfully lay siege to Béthune.

At about this time Queen Anne was engaged in ridding herself of her Whig Ministry with its policy of continuing the European war. Gradually Whig ministers were replaced by men from the Tory ranks, the most notable substitution being that of Robert Harley for Lord Godolphin. Parliament was subsequently dissolved and a general election called for October. This resulted in a massive Tory victory with 320 seats to the Whigs' 150, with 40 undecided. Notwithstanding this crushing Whig defeat, Cadogan retained his seat at Woodstock. At the close of the campaign in November, with the costs of the war seeming to be never-ending and with the mounting casualty lists, there appeared a strong possibility that at last a Tory Ministry would succeed in finding a peace formula with King Louis.

Cadogan joined Marlborough at the Hague and stayed there until the Duke's departure for England in the last days of December. He then returned to Brussels where he received a letter from Henry Boyle, one of the Queen's ministers, conveying Her Majesty's commands for his recall. Cadogan replied on the 5th January that

As I have been established in this place these three years with my family and that I did not expect to be removed without some warning, I shall be obliged to stay tho' without a character, a fortnight at least for the settling of my private affairs. If Mr. Hill arrives during that time, I shall endeavour to give him all the light I can into the business here, especially that part which may relate to the forwarding our preparations for the early taking the field.

Cadogan's replacement was to be Brigadier Jack Hill, brother of the Queen's new favourite Mrs Masham who had replaced the erstwhile favourite, Sarah, the Duchess of Marlborough. At the same time there was a rumour in Court circles that the brigadier would also in due time replace Cadogan as Lieutenant of the Tower of London. Marlborough's power was ebbing fast and Cadogan's loss of his diplomatic post was a foretaste of things to come.

The Tory Ministry, notwithstanding their dislike of Marlborough, offered him command of the English army for a further campaign and having accepted, the Duke wrote to Heinsius the Grand Pensionary of Holland on the 6th February 1711 that 'I have write to Cadogan that that he should take with you at the Hague the necessary measures for the army's taking the field earlyer this year than the last . . .' So it was that by the end of April the Allied army of 142 battalions and 269 squadrons, amounting to close on 120,000 troops, had gathered under Marlborough near to Douai. The French army for the coming campaign was again to be commanded by Marshal Villars and he had under his orders a force of 160 battalions and 244 squadrons. During the winter months the French had constructed, so as to protect their interior, a formidable barrier some ninety miles in length stretching from the River Canche on the Channel coast to Namur on the River Sambre, making use of the natural terrain and supplementing this with earth-works and palisades. The barrier was supported by a number of major fortresses including Arras, Bouchain and

Cambrai and according to Villars this line of defence, known as 'the lines', was the 'Non Plus Ultra' of the Duke. In other words Marlborough would be stopped here.

The campaign was slow to get under way and it was not until the middle of June that the Captain-General gave the orders which resulted, on the 6th July, in the taking of Arleux nine miles west of the Bouchain fortress and close to the lines. The move was a subterfuge to unsettle and goad the French and Marlborough's main aim was to secure the area around Arleux so as to give him eventual access for the investment of Bouchain. Villars duly responded to the Allied challenge and on the 11th July he launched an assault on Arleux. Cadogan was despatched at the head of thirty squadrons and a force of grenadiers, but he seemed to have orders to make haste slowly and in the event Arleux was retaken by the enemy. As if smarting under this loss Marlborough then moved his army, seemingly to attack the lines in the vicinity of Arras, and on the 4th August he rode out under escort to inspect the French position.

Included in the Duke's party was a Captain Parker and he noticed 'General Cadogan steal out of the crowd attended by one servant only', but 'did not think much of this circumstance at that time'.[9] Cadogan was in fact heading for Douai to make rendezvous with the Allied General Hompesch where the two soldiers would assume joint-command of a vanguard of 20 battalions and 17 squadrons. From Douai the force descended upon Arleux to find it and the enemy's lines beyond deserted. By the middle of the next day the whole of Marlborough's army had followed where Cadogan and Hompesch had lead the way. The French had been completely taken by surprise and the lines of Non Plus Ultra breached. The Allies were now ready for a grand battle, but not so the French who withdrew south to Cambrai. Marlborough did not seek to force the issue and the Allied army went on, in accordance with his original design, to lay siege to Bouchain. This proved to be another bloody business and it was thirty-four days before the fortress capitulated on the 13th September. 'Marlborough was Master of Bouchain. It was his last conquest and command.'[10]

From his camp at Bouchain Cadogan, in evident admiration of his Commander, wrote on the 14th September 1711 to Mr. James Craggs[11] at Whitehall

I should make a great many excuses for the freedom I take in troubling you, were it on any other occasion than this of acquainting you with the happy conclusion of the siege of Bouchain, which has been attended by all the circumstances My Lord Duke's friends could wish for his glory and reputation. His Grace undertook it in sight of the enemy army, tho'

The 2nd Duke of Ormonde   *James Craggs*

superior to his by above 30 battalions, and commanded by a general that France looked on as its last hope and who, piqued even to rage by being duped in the passage of the Lines, was resolved to leave nothing unattempted to repair his fault and relieve Bouchain. He indeed made a great many efforts towards it, but they all proved fruitless by the measures His Grace took to disappoint them, so that notwithstanding the French army's remaining within cannon shot of our approaches, yet our convoys of bread and artillery came regularly and safe, our communication was preserved with our great towns, and in 15 days after our batteries began to fire, the place was surrendered and the garrison consisting of eight battalions and a detachment of 600 Swiss [Guards] made Prisoners of War.[12]

The States-General were now tiring of the war and they showed their disinclination to give further support to Marlborough. Accordingly, having garrisoned Bouchain, he withdrew to Tournai and soon afterwards left for the Hague. From there, on the 13th November, he addressed an order to Cadogan: 'Whereas upon my return to England and during my absence the Command-in-Chief of Her Majesty's forces in the Low Countrys will devolve to you . . .' On his return home Marlborough learned that a Parliamentary Commission had been set up to look into alleged irregularities concerning money he had received from the army's bread and transport contractors and a percentage he had received from the payment of foreign auxiliaries. It became clear that whatever the validity of Marlborough's defence, the Tory Ministry would secure his downfall and on the 11th January 1712 the Queen declared in Council the Duke's immediate dismissal. All Marlborough's official appointments at once became void and the Duke of Ormonde became Captain-General. Cadogan now had a new commander.

[73]

CHAPTER VII

Resignations and Reinstatement

The news of Marlborough's dismissal sent shock waves round Europe and raised French hopes of an early peace. There was a feeling of disquiet in the army and Cadogan writing from Brussels expressed his concern at length in a letter to the Duke dated the 20th January 1712.

My Concern and astonishment att the fatal news of Your Graces being removed are as hard to be expressed as the terror and consternation it has struck all people with here. Everything is in the utmost confusion, and every honest man looks on the Common Cause as irrevocably lost. By the same hand Your Grace receives this letter I send to Mr. Cardonnel [Marlborough's secretary] certificates and attestations concerning the business of the bread. For these five and thirty years past, it was an established custom to present the General commanding in Chief with a considerable annual gratification in proportion to the number of troops the army was composed of. One of these certificates is signed by Cardosa who lives att Brussels, and was partner with Vonseas Father in the two preceding wars, the other is signed by Marcada who was Book-keeper and Cash-keeper to old Perera and Machada in the last war, and partner with Machada in the beginning of this . . . Your Graces Letter of the 1st of this month o.s. did not come to my hands till last night. Monsieur Slingeland, under whose cover it was sent, gave it to my wife who believing it to be of moment, forwarded it by express to Brussells, the express missed me on the way so that I did not receive it till yesterday the 19th n.s. and it was consequently impossible for me to get into England by the 10th o.s. besides, there is a strict order given the Masters of the paquet boats to take no person of what character soever on board, without my Lord Straffords Passeport which I was privately informed would be refused me. As to the letter Your Grace mentions to have sent me with leave to come into England, I have not as yet received it, for which I can imagine no other reason but its being stopt in the Post Office. I shall therefore wait here till the return of this messenger by whom I hope Your Grace will send me your commands in relation to what I am to doe. I persuade myself 'tis unnecessary to repeat the assurances of my intention to follow Your Grace in all fortunes, in order to which my resolution is to leave the Service and I can only defer it, till I receive Your Graces directions concerning the manner I am to doe it, whether I should write to the Secretary of State for a permission to come over on account of my private affairs, then lay down, or whether I should write from this side for immediate leave to quit. I conclude that a Permission of some kind (since Your Graces Leave has not come to my hands) is absolutely necessary, otherwise they may bring me to a Council of War for quitting without licence the command Your Grace entrusted me with.

To ensure the delivery of his letter Cadogan sent it 'by a gentleman of the Portugal Ambassadors whom he is so kind as to send on purpose, under pretence of carrying letters to the Prince [Eugène] of Savoy, to whom this paquet for the greater security is addressed'. Cadogan concludes his letter 'I have nothing else to add but my most ardent prayers and vows for Your Graces prosperity . . .'[1]

Cadogan was clearly still perturbed four days later when, returned to the Hague, he wrote to a friend

Wee have dear Judge in the course of our long acquaintance generally agreed in our opinions of men and things, this makes it easy for me to guess att the indisposition of mind you complain of, and the cause of it. I am deeply affected in the same part, and by the same distemper, and

am so far gone in it, as not only to be tired of business and employments, but even weary of life itself. You know the bottome of my
heart, therefore can better imagine then I describe the affliction and
weight of grief I am under. I am uncertain and I assure you unconcerned
as to what becomes of myself. I shall act according to the strictest rules
of gratitude duty and honour, in relation to our great unfortunate
benefactor, [Marlborough] and my zeal inclination and desire to serve
and suffer for him are equal to the vast obligations and favours I have
received from him. As to the rest, I shall doe as people att sea when the
violence of the storm obliges them to abandon the helm and cut down
the masts, I commit my self to the mercy of the winds and waves.
Whether they force me to split on rocks or whether my good fortune
may throw a plank in my way to carry me ashore, I am grown so
insensible or so resigned as to be no longer in pain about.[2]

The 'certificates and attestations' sent to Marlborough by
Cadogan were to no avail and in late January the House of
Commons voted by 265 to 155 in favour of a motion that
the Duke had illegally taken commission on the bread
money and, further, that the percentage he had received on
the payment of foreign auxiliaries should be investigated.

In the event Cadogan was not recalled to England by
Marlborough who, on the contrary, expressed a wish that
he should continue to serve as one of Her Majesty's generals
in the Allied army. Accordingly Cadogan then offered
his services as Quartermaster-General to Ormonde who
accepted. Marlborough was probably not being entirely
altruistic in leaving Cadogan in Flanders for the new campaign as this gave him a prime source of continental intelligence. In this role Cadogan, 'that trusted eye',[3] wrote to
Marlborough on the 10th March describing the success of a
plan to obstruct the enemy by burning the magazine at
Arras and mining the River Sambre, which meant that the

French could not take the field before the end of May. As it transpired it was unnecessary for the enemy to leave camp at all, at least as far as the British army was concerned, for as a result of secret Anglo-French negotiations Ormonde was issued with 'restraining orders' on the 10th May by which he was forbidden to use British troops against the French. Cadogan therefore had only the supply problems of the British army to occupy him as the campaign of 1712 gradually ground to a halt with the remainder of the Allied army under Prince Eugène suffering badly at the hands of the French, commanded again by Villars. The Dutch now realised that they could not continue the war without England and in the following year there came about the Peace of Utrecht, a series of treaties which officially ended the War of the Spanish Succession. Under the 'Peace' Britain gained Hudson Bay, Arcadia and Newfoundland from the French and Gibraltar, Minorca and colonial trading concessions from Spain. The United Provinces received a limited Barrier, Prussia and Savoy gained Upper Guelderland and Sicily respectively and Portugal some trading rights in South America. By virtue of the two major treaties both France and Spain recognised the Hanoverian succession and Louis' grandson in turn was recognised as King Philip V of Spain on the understanding that he renounced his rights to the French throne. Negotiated by a Tory administration, the treaties were regarded by the Whigs as a betrayal of Britain's Allies and they were passed by Parliament only with difficulty. This notwithstanding, the end of the Spanish War achieved for the Grand Alliance one of its main aims: the Spanish inheritance had been kept apart from France and in addition a balance of power in Europe

[77]

attained. Britain, as a result of the war, was to emerge as a great world power.

In the meantime Marlborough had continued to attend the House of Lords to make known his views but as 1712 drew on, 'it became increasingly evident that he would be well-advised to leave the country in his own interests'.[4] There were a number of reasons for this, primarily perhaps the need for a spell of peace and quiet away from the hubbub of British politics. In early December therefore the Duke took the paquet-boat from Dover to Ostend accompanied by a few servants. To ensure his financial security during his exile Marlborough had earlier transferred £50,000 to Cadogan at the Hague and at the same time he had written to the Lord Treasurer, Robert Harley, Earl of Oxford, requesting that Cadogan be released from his duties to enable him to travel with Marlborough. Cadogan also wrote to Lord Oxford 'The Duke of Marlborough's ill health and the inconvenience a winters journey exposes him to and his being without any friend to accompany him, makes the requesting leave to wait on him an indispensable duty on me who, for so many years have been honoured with his confidence and friendship, and owe all I have in the world to his favour.' The Tory Ministry responded with a call for Cadogan to resign all his offices and employments under the Crown and as a result of this he sold the colonelcy of his regiment to Major-General Kellum, a veteran who had served with the Sixth Horse since its first formation in 1685, for £3000.[5] Cadogan then followed Marlborough into exile and took up residence at the Manor of Raaphorst, a 520-acre estate in the district of Wassenaar situated about ten miles from the Hague. Mrs Cadogan won the estate in a

Raaphorst Castle

lottery in 1712 although the prize was burdened with a debt of 40,000 guilders which the Cadogans had to redeem. The manorial seat was Raaphorst Castle, a gloomy looking gothic-style building with turrets and tall chimneys. General and Mrs. Cadogan who by now had a second daughter Margaret, leased another much smaller estate nearby called 'De Drie Papagaaien' (The Three Parrots).

After visiting Aix-la-Chapelle Marlborough travelled to Frankfurt where he took up residence. Cadogan visited him frequently and spent a great deal of time 'away upon the road' as the Duke's agent in London, Hanover and the Hague. In December 1713 Queen Anne became seriously ill and there was plotting within the Tory administration in defiance of the Act of Settlement to effect a Jacobite restoration on the Queen's death. Marlborough flirted with this idea for a time and even corresponded with the Old Pretender, son of James II. In the final event, however, he came down on the side of Hanover and Cadogan, who also spoke

German,[6] was a frequent visitor on Marlborough's behalf to the Court of the Elector. The Queen recovered and the question of the succession became less urgent. In June 1714 Sophia, the 84-year-old Electress of Hanover died and her son George, the Elector, became Heir Apparent to the childless Queen Anne who by now had suffered a relapse. To counter the Tory plot, which if successful would have caused a civil war in Britain, George adopted a plan suggested by his foreign affairs adviser, Count Bernstorff. To enable him to assume control immediately on the Queen's death Marlborough was to become Captain-General and try to secure the allegiance of the British troops at Bruges, Ghent and Dunkirk. Cadogan meanwhile was to go to London, sieze the Tower and administer the oath of allegiance to the troops serving in the home army. To ensure there were no difficulties in the case of an emergency, George issued undated commissions to Marlborough and Cadogan so that they could take command at short notice.[7]

They waited to see what developments took place but when the Duke of Berwick, one of Louis' marshals, left France for Spain Marlborough became convinced that there would be no Jacobite invasion in the near future and left his home (now in Antwerp) for England in late July. When Marlborough, now accompanied by Cadogan, arrived at Dover on the 2nd August they learned that the Queen had died the previous day. The transfer of sovereignty from the Stuarts to the House of Hanover went without any overt move on the part of the Pretender and the Elector's plan was not implemented. King George I landed in his new country at Greenwich on the 18th September and the first royal warrant signed by him reinstated Marlborough as Captain-

General. Cadogan did not go unrewarded and he was reinstated in his former rank of Lieutenant-General and was also appointed Master of the King's Robes, Lieutenant of the Ordnance and Colonel of the Coldstream Guards, the latter appointment being dated the 11th August 1714. He was also accredited as Envoy Extraordinary and Minister Plenipotentiary to the States-General of Holland and re-chosen for the fifth time as Member of Parliament for the borough of Woodstock.

As if in anticipation of these events Cadogan on the 3rd July, less than a month before the death of the Queen, had taken a 99 years' lease on the Caversham Estate close to Reading in Berkshire, from Elizabeth Countess Dowager of Kildare at a rent of £200 per annum together with 'One Brace of Fat Bucks and One Brace of Fat Does'.[8] The estate extended to just over 1,000 acres and included a mansion house, Caversham Lodge, and a great deer park of 240 acres.[9] Caversham was a much grander proposition than the Manor of Oakley and it was ideally situated, having within a forty-mile radius the Duke of Marlborough's Palace at Blenheim and the Royal Courts at Windsor and London. Cadogan had become a considerable man of property for in addition to his interests in Holland and England he also now owned estates in Ireland following the death of his father Henry on the 13th January 1714. Although Henry's will has not survived it seems that the bulk of the family's lands were bequeathed to William as the elder son with a smaller interest being allotted to his younger brother Charles. The year had been a successful one for Cadogan who was now restored to royal favour. Good fortune had indeed thrown him a plank and carried him ashore.

[81]

CHAPTER VIII

Rebellion in Scotland

During the early months of 1715 Cadogan travelled frequently between Antwerp, Brussels, the Hague and Vienna in his rôle as the British representative in negotiations between Britain, the Empire and Holland relating to a new Barrier Treaty for the better protection of the United Provinces against any future French expansionism. He won a further mark of royal favour on the 31st July when he was chosen to succeed General Webb, the victor of Wynendael, as Governor of Carisbrooke Castle and Captain of the Isle of Wight. The appointment carried with it the offices of Steward, Surveyor, Receiver and Bailiff of all mansions, lands, tenements, woods, heriditaments and other revenues within the Island. It was a lucrative office with 'All Rights, Powers, Privileges and Advantages thereunto respectively belonging to William Cadogan by himself or his Deputys for and during the term of his natural life'. Cadogan's first official engagement in his new appointment occurred on the 27th September at Carisbrooke Castle, when he received members of the Island's Council. During his continental travels Cadogan continued to gather military and political intelligence, not on this occasion for Marlborough but for his masters in London. This is evidenced by a money warrant for £1,500 dated the 19th August which followed a Royal Sign Manual issued by the Treasury, 'to William Cadogan Envoy Extraordinary and Plenipotentiary to the States-General and at the Congress at Antwerp, the same being intended to repay him the like sum which he has disbursed for secret intelligence by our particular order'.

In Scotland meanwhile, the Jacobites, disappointed at the succession of George I, were once again plotting to put the Pretender on the throne as James VIII. They had found themselves a new leader in the person of a Scottish nobleman, the Earl of Mar, who had been one of the chief men in carrying through the Act of Union but who had afterwards changed his mind and voted against it. Lord Mar had at first tried to gain favour with George but when this failed he determined to raise a rebellion against him in Scotland with the aim of bringing back the Stuarts. In early August therefore Mar, disguised as a workman, went aboard a coal-sloop in the Thames and sailed to Fife where he endeavoured to raise the Jacobites. He then travelled to his own lands in Aberdeenshire where he arranged a great deer hunt to which he invited those Highland chiefs who were given to the Stuart cause. As a result of this meeting of the chiefs it was agreed that on the 7th September the standard would be raised for King James. On that day Mar, with a force of some sixty men, raised the standard at Castleton in Braemar. The rebellion had begun. Mar then marched southwards and was joined on the way by many nobles and chiefs with their followers. The town of Perth soon fell to the Jacobite army which by now numbered some 9000 men.[1]

When the news reached London Cadogan was deeply

engrossed in finalising the Barrier Treaty negotiations. This notwithstanding, however, he was immediately ordered by Lord Townshend, secretary of state for the northern department in the new Whig administration, to the Hague to seek from the States-General 6000 Dutch and Swiss troops for service in Scotland. At the Hague Cadogan met the Deputies for Foreign Affairs and formally presented the *memoire* by which King George asked that these troops be embarked for England. The request was granted and the responsibility for equipping the expedition fell upon Cadogan who tackled the matter with his usual zest. The troops were in a state of readiness before the end of October and Cadogan went to Antwerp to make arrangements for their embarkation. From there he reported to Lord Townshend that orders had been sent to all regiments to march speedily for the Channel port of Ostend. The regiments furthest away were at Maastricht but they would arrive by the 10th November. In the meantime the ships, provisions and other necessaries would be prepared. Cadogan concluded his report with news received from Lord Stair, the British ambassador in Paris. The Pretender had resolved to proceed to Britain and if refused permission to pass through France would attempt together with his aides to travel by way of countries bordering on Holland. 'I have requested the States-General to issue very exact orders to examine all persons who arrive at their seaports and to forbid Masters of Ships to receive on board any subject of His Majesty without a passport signed by my hand.' Cadogan then made a visit to Brussels; from there he travelled to the Hague for the signing of the Barrier Treaty on the 15th November.

The 2nd Duke of Argyll   The 6th Earl of Mar

On completion of his diplomatic mission Cadogan set out for Ostend where he sailed with the convoy taking the Dutch and Swiss troops to London, disembarking at the beginning of December. They then journeyed north, reaching Stirling two weeks later. Cadogan now established contact with the Duke of Argyll who at the outset of the rebellion had been appointed Commander-in-Chief of the King's forces in Scotland which numbered about 3000 men. Although born in England the Duke was a Scottish nobleman and he had served under Marlborough during the recent war, fighting with distinction at the battles of Ramillies and Malplaquet and rising to the rank of Lieutenant-General.

After the campaign of 1709 Marlborough, not for the first time, had let it be known to Queen Anne that he felt it would be appropriate if he were to be appointed Captain-

General for life. Argyll had his own martial ambitions and was opposed along with others to this proposal, so from this point on he worked for Marlborough's overthrow. During Queen Anne's ultimate illness in 1714, Argyll together with the Duke of Somerset had intervened at the last Council, proposing the Duke of Shrewsbury as Lord Treasurer. This appointment ensured the failure of Jacobite plans to gain the throne for the Pretender and in consequence Argyll was held in high regard by King George who appointed him to his command.

On his arrival in Scotland in mid-September 1715, Argyll marshalled his troops at Stirling to prevent Mar from bringing his army across the River Forth. Lord Mar eventually took the initiative and led his men south to meet Argyll at Sheriffmuir on the 24th November. The ground formation was such that the two armies were hidden from each other for a time and when battle was joined it was found that they were not directly opposed. The outcome was a victory claimed by both sides on the right wing, but Argyll obtained the overall advantage as, on the following morning, Mar's army was not to be seen. Lord Mar subsequently sent an enquiry to Argyll as to his power to grant terms and he in turn asked the Government for powers to treat. No notice was taken of his communication and this lack of response probably cooled Argyll's enthusiasm for the task. On the other hand, although the Pretender had at last reached the rebels' camp at Perth, the Highlanders were already beginning to desert their leader. Following Sheriffmuir Argyll, perhaps out of sympathy for his fellow Scots, pursued a policy of strict containment and did not attempt a march on Perth. It was this lack of prosecution in the campaign which lead Marlborough as Captain-General to instruct Cadogan, second-in-command to Argyll, to maintain a discreet watching brief on his commander.

Cadogan reported to Marlborough from Edinburgh on the 19th December:

I have writt the enclosed in French that if your Grace thinks proper it may be shown the King. The Duke of Argyle intends to stay, but with what view, a very little time will explain, for his past conduct, his present aims, and his national temper give but so much reason to apprehend he will by indirect and underhand means, endeavour to obstruct and disappoint every thing I shall propose . . . He [Argyll] carrys very civilly to me in appearance, but in reality, is more employed and busied in finding out means to make every thing miscarry that I should undertake, than he is to act against the Rebels. I receive no manner of assistance or advice but from the Justice Clerk Lord Rothies Lord Hadington and Sir John Anstruther. This difficult situation puts me on my guard as much as possible, and will render the having all the information can be sent me from London more necessary than ever, to which end I hope your Grace will find it proper, that extracts of what he writes to the Secretary of State, and the instructions and orders he receives, should be communicated to me. As to the rest I think every thing easy, and I even beleive My Lord Mar will abandon Perth when wee approach it. He has now three thousand men and can never assemble above five. All imaginable pains is taken by the Duke of Argyle and his friends to magnify the courage of the Highlanders and to speak ill of our troops, which coming from the Generals has had a very ill effect on the men. I have therefore been as industrious to reassure them, and have on all occasions endeavoured to make them condemn these formidable Clans as an undisciplined rabble, and unable to fight with troops used to victory for so many years under your Grace . . . The Postmaster of Edinburgh is a creature of the Duke of Argyles and opens all letters. When your Grace has therefore any thing in particular to write to me, it may be addressed to the Postmaster at Berwick . . .

[87]

From the report 'in French' it is evident that Cadogan took north with him a letter from Lord Townshend containing an order from King George 'pour mettre fin à la Rebellion le plus promptement qu'il sera possible'. Cadogan makes it clear that in his view the Duke of Argyll 'is not thinking of taking action before next summer' and that in any event 'most of Argyles officers do not have the tents or horses necessary for a winter campaign'.[2] In the light of subsequent events it is most likely that the King did see Cadogan's report.

On the 31st December Cadogan wrote again to Marlborough and was able to report on a much improved situation:

The Duke of Argyle has just now told me he had by last post acquainted the Secretary of State, that he approved of the project I sent and would march about the 12th Jan. to put it in execution . . . the Country is everywhere so full of corn that your Grace may depend on it, wee shall never be embarrased for our subsistence. The Duke of Argyle likewise said to me, leave had been given him to goe to London, but with such restrictions and so many ifs, as he termed it, that he could make no use of it, he added that no consideration whatsoever should prevail on him to stay longer than till the business of Perth was over ... [Cadogan concludes on a personal note] I have been ill these three or four days past of a flux which was the reason of my missing last post, but am, God be thanked, now so well as to be able to goe out to morrow.[3]

From the comments ascribed to Argyll it now seemed that the way was paved for Cadogan to take over command in Scotland.

As events transpired, the march on Perth did not begin until the 21st January 1716. It was a difficult manoeuvre, for the enemy had burned all the villages on the way so that the

The march on Perth

troops had to take with them provisions for twelve days. The problem of haulage was made the more demanding as the countryside lay deep in snow which had to be cleared by gangs of labourers as they proceeded. On the 30th January as the royalist force approached the town, Lord Mar and his army, now led by the Pretender, departed from Perth, marching first to Dundee and thence to Montrose. Cadogan had been right in his assessment of the situation and the rebels had chosen not to fight. At Montrose the friends of the Pretender persuaded him that it was no longer safe to remain in Scotland and so, unknown to their army, he and Mar and some others slipped away in the darkness and sailed for France. The rebels deserted by their leaders soon dispersed, each man 'taking the road that pleased him best'. The rebellion of 1715 was now broken and all that remained was to hunt down the fleeing rebels and bring the remaining leaders to book. By the 21st February Cadogan had reached Aberdeen and from here he wrote to Marlborough: 'The very great civility the Duke of Argyle shews the Rebels who surrender, and the very little care taken to seise or apprehend any, tho not only the Country, but this very Town is full of them surprises every body who wishes well the Kings service.'[4]

On the 23rd February, still in Aberdeen, Cadogan again reported to the Captain-General and it was with evident relief that he was able to record that the Duke of Argyll had now been recalled to London.

I think I may venture to assure your Grace, that in a month after the Duke of Argyle leaves this Kingdom, the Rebels will be reduced to submit all of them att discretion. The advices I last had from the Highlands say the Chiefs of the Clans and the principal gentlemen will endeavour to get in to France, and conceal themselves till they have an opportunity of doing it, and that the Common People will give up their arms, and throw themselves on the Kings mercy.

Cadogan goes on to say that he is formulating a plan to reduce the rebels after which 'your Grace may depend on it, this Rebellion shall be plucked up by the roots, and no seeds left for another'.[5] Cadogan now campaigned south-westwards and on the 31st March, having taken over command from the Duke of Argyll, he writes to Marlborough from his camp at the Blair of Athol that 'Since my arrival here with the Troops, all the Rebels in these Parts have brought in their arms and surrendered att discretion, which they have likewise done in the several places where I have sent detachments. I . . . hope in a fortnight to finish every thing in the manner your Grace directed.' He adds, 'The Scotch officers who deserted the Dutch service will be executed in effigy next week in Edinburgh.'[6]

By the 10th April Cadogan had reached Inverness, the northernmost point in his campaign, and from here he was able to report to Marlborough that 'all the Clans have submitted except Lord Seaforth's and Macdonald's of the Isles', who he anticipated would 'come in as the others had done, and would deliver their arms by Saturday next'. Cadogan had also gained some intelligence on the rebellion conspiracy:

Glengary surrendered himself last night, and I have sent him prisoner to Perth. He discovered to me all he knew concerning the rise and progress of the Rebellion and told me honestly what had past in relation to the money given the Clans by the Earl of Oxford . . . it was transacted att London between my Lord Oxford and the Earl of Mar, and that he believed the only Persons immediately trusted by the Earl of Oxford in the matter, were the Earl of Mar, the Earl of Kinoul, and My lord Duplin.[7]

[Eight days later the indefatigable Cadogan again put pen to paper to advise Marlborough that] Having now seen all the places in Scotland where it may be proper to erect forts and redoubts, for keeping the Highlanders in subjection and securing the quiet and tranquility of the Kingdom in general, I directed the Engineers with me, in persuance of your Graces Orders, to make plans of the fortifications that will be necessary, and estimates of what they will cost, which I shall get ready in a post or two, to send your Grace, as likewise a project concerning the number of troops it may be requisite to leave here in the time of Peace.[8]

From Inverness Cadogan then made his way south, stopping off at Aberdeen and Perth. On the 11th May he was in Edinburgh writing his final report of the campaign to Marlborough:

I have received the Honour of your Graces letter of the 1st with his Majestys permission for returning into England, as soon as his service would allow of it, and as there is not a single Rebel now in arms, and that the public peace and tranquility is restored in all parts of the Kingdom I judged it unnecessary for me to stay any longer, and intend therefore to begin my journey to morrow towards London. I have given orders to the Dutch troops to march into England, and sent copys of the routes to the Secretary att War. I flatter my self with the satisfaction of seeing your Grace very soon, tis the greatest I can have in the world.[9]

CHAPTER IX

Honours and a Formal Entry

It was probably no surprise to the able Cadogan when
Marlborough broached the matter of his advancement
to the nobility. Cadogan in his letter to the Duke from
Aberdeen dated the 23rd February 1716 writes:

Your Grace having been pleased to order me to let you know the name
of the Barony I desire to be called by, att the same time I beg your Grace
to accept of my most sincere thanks for this new and distinguishing
mark of your favour and protection, I presume to acquaint you, the
place I propose is called Cadogan near Wrexham on the borders of
Wales, of the Cheshire side, and as I am not so happy as to have a son,
and that in case I should not, I have settled a great part of my fortune on
my Brother (Charles), it would be an infinite satisfaction to me, if the
title was limited to him, should I leave no male issue, but if your Grace
judges this not reasonable to ask, or that there will be any difficulty in
obtaining it, I humbly beg pardon for mentioning it, and entreat your
Grace would consider it no more than if I had not.[1]

Cadogan's proposal did not find immediate favour and
when he was granted his Letters Patent on the 21st June
1716 he was created Lord Cadogan, Baron of Reading in the
County of Berkshire, with no remainder for his brother.
The preamble to his patent initially sets forth in high-flown
phrase Lord Cadogan's virtues and then goes on to praise
his military and diplomatic prowess:

[93]

In the exploits of war, an undaunted bravery and a greatness of soul have, upon every occasion shone forth in the brightest light, particularly in the late war against France, conducted by the wisdom and magnanimity of the most illustrious John, Duke of Marlborough; with a glory, which hath made his name outshine all the heroes of antiquity, and will render it the wonder of posterity; A war, in which, through the course of ten years, the cause of true religion, of the universal liberty of our own countries, and the countries of our allies, of all right and law, contended against the open attempts of tyrany and slavery. A war prosecuted with so resolute and determined a zeal, that not only the summer, but even the winter itself was seldom free from action; and always attended with such unparalleled success, that, through that whole time, no one battle was fought which was not gained, no one town besieged which was not gloriously taken: in that war, carried on with so unequalled a glory, under the conduct and command of so consummate a general, he bore a faithful and unwearied part both in the councils of the cabinet, and in the labours of the field.

Afterwards, in the late war at home, against the madness of the most unnatural rebels and traitors, in the heart of winter, in the midst of the most piercing frosts and deepest snows, he shewed a conduct and an application in the highest degree faithful, and in the most signal manner successful.

And lastly, in the late treaty for fixing such towns and fortresses, as might be truly a barrier to the United Provinces, our ever faithful and inseparable allies; he manifested such a constancy of attention, such a regard to right and justice, such a dexterity in business, as is very seldom equalled, never exceeded. And this with so good effect, that it may justly be said to have once more revived and established the ancient friendship and intercourse of good offices between Great Britain, and not only the United Provinces, but also the most serene and august house of Austria. Upon all which accounts, moved by his own great merits, and assured of the approbation of all good men, we have resolved to promote him into the rank of our Peers.[2]

In further recognition of his service in Scotland, Cadogan was appointed a Knight of the Most Ancient and Most

The Order of the Thistle

Noble Order of the Thistle, the Scottish Order of Knighthood which ranks only second to the Garter in the list of British Orders. He took his oath in the presence of the King and his brother Knights at an investiture held in St James's Palace on the 22nd June. This was the first occasion on which an English peer was so honoured. At about this time he was also appointed High Steward of Reading. During early July there came advancement in his diplomatic career when it was announced that Lord Cadogan was to return to the Hague as Ambassador Extraordinary and Plenipotentiary. In this capacity he turned his thoughts to the trappings of office and he applied to the Lords of the Treasury for furnishings for the State Chapel in the Embassy. A Treasury subscription for execution of a Warrant dated the 19th July was accordingly sent by the Duke of Bolton, Lord Chamberlain of the Household to the Duke of Montagu, Master of the Great Wardrobe, to deliver to Lord Cadogan a 'cloth of state of crimson damask with gold and silver fringe, a chair, two stools, two cushions, a footstool and foot carpet as usual, a large Bible of Imperial paper richly bound in two volumes, four Common Prayer Books in

[95]

quarto, an altar cloth of tissue pan'l with velvet, twenty els of fine diaper for towels, and two large surplices of fine Holland'.

Cadogan duly returned to the Hague by way of Brussels and on the 15th September he signed the treaty of defensive alliance between Great Britain, France and Holland. He presented his credentials on the 7th October and then attended King George on a visit to Hanover. A further mark of royal favour was accorded Cadogan on the 17th March 1717 when he was sworn of the Privy Council. There was now, however, a cloud on the horizon and on the 4th June a 'vexatious indictment'[3] was brought against him in the House of Commons by Tory Jacobites to whom his success in Scotland was anathema. The Charge, supported by Sir Robert Walpole, was that Cadogan had defrauded the government in connection with the transport of the Dutch and Swiss troops to England during the rising in the north. Lord Stanhope and other eminent Whigs spoke at the bar of the House in support of Cadogan and the motion was defeated, so deflating Jacobite expectations that he would be 'roasted in the House of Commons'. Happier events now took Cadogan's attention and on the 12th July he was constituted General of all his Majesty's Foot Guards. Later in the month he was witness to his brother's marriage to Elizabeth Sloane at the church of St. George the Martyr in Queen Square, London. Charles Cadogan was now commissioned lieutenant-colonel in the Coldstream Guards and in the previous year under Lord Cadogan's patronage he had been elected Member of Parliament for Reading. Elizabeth was the younger daughter of a very wealthy and fashionable Irish physician, Sir Hans Sloane,

Sir Robert Walpole,
1st Earl of Orford

Sir Hans Sloane

who was also Lord of the Manor of Chelsea. Sir Hans was one of the physicians who treated Queen Anne in her last illness.

When in London, Lord Cadogan now resided in a house in the newly built Hanover Square.[4] With the approach of autumn he returned to the Embassy at the Hague but he came back to London at the opening of 1718 to closely follow a Bill introduced into the House of Commons on the 4th February for 'regulating the forces to be continued in His Majestys service, for the payment of the said forces and their quarters, and for punishing mutiny and desertion'. When the Bill came before the House of Lords, Cadogan was one of the speakers in a great debate opened by the Earl of Oxford who, following Cadogan's intelligence gathering during the rebellion of 1715, had recently spent some time incarcerated in the Tower of London. Cadogan's old commander the Duke of Argyll averred, 'that besides the 16,000 and odd men of regular troops, there was another considerable body maintained under the denomination of invalids.' This drew forth a rejoinder from Cadogan that, 'he knew no invalids but such as were in Chelsea Colledge [presumably a reference to Chelsea Hospital] or the neighbourhood.' Later in the debate the question was raised as to whether the maintenance of a 'standing army in peace would rather increase then lessen the enemies of the Government'. Cadogan confidently asserted, 'that if the Army was reduced to 12,000 men, it were impossible upon any emergency to assemble a body of 4,000 men in any part of Great Britain besides London, without leaving the sea ports and other important Posts, unguarded.'

Three months later on the 8th May Lord Cadogan was advanced to the dignity of Baron of Oakley, Viscount Caversham and Earl of Cadogan with remainder of the barony of Oakley to his brother Charles Cadogan. The preamble to his new patent sets out that:

Whereas we thought fit, about two years since, to give the rank and dignity of a Peer of this realm to William, Lord Cadogan, by the title of Baron of Reading, in consideration of his great and eminent services; and particularly those performed by him during the war in Flanders, and after that, in the late rebellion in Scotland, as is more fully set forth in the preamble of our patent for creating him Baron of Reading; and we having great reason to be extremely satisfied with the services he has since done in several important negotiations transacted by him, as our Ambassador extraordinary in Holland; and with his conduct and behaviour in his station of General of our foot, and Commander of our forces next under the Duke of Marlborough; and he having continued to give us upon all occasions, and in the most difficult times, singular

The Right Honourable William Lord Cadogan Lieutenant General of His Majesty's Forces &c.ᵃ

Pro Patriâ Constans, Generosus, Fidus amicis │ Si Laurum Cœleste Decus, si Sydera quæras
Invictus bello: Gallia tota tumet. │ Hujusce Eximij, sint tua facta Viri.

Laguerre pinx: Simon fecit & ex:

The 1st Earl Cadogan

and undoubted proofs of his zeal for our service, and of his steady, firm, inviolable, and unalterable affection to our person and government; and we having farther an intention to send him speedily into Holland, to negotiate with the States General their entering into the alliance between ourselves, the Emperor, and the French King; which is an affair of the utmost consequence to the good of these our kingdoms in particular, and of Europe in general; and we having likewise given him orders to make a public entry, in quality of our Ambassador extraordinary at the Hague, to assure the States, in the most solemn manner, of our constant friendship and affection to their commonwealth. For these reasons, and to give a greater lustre and dignity to the commission we now employ him in, we have thought fit to confer upon him a new degree of honour, and to create him Earl of Cadogan, in Denbighshire; Viscount of Caversham, in Oxfordshire; and Baron of Oakley, in Buckinghamshire.[5]

Cadogan's earlier proposal to the Duke of Marlborough had now been accepted and he had ensured that in the absence of his having a son, one of his titles, the barony of Oakley, would pass to his brother. His wish to relate a title to a 'Place . . . called Cadogan' had also been granted and this is intriguing because at the time there appears to have been no such place sufficient to have supported a territorial title. Cadogan seems to have mistranslated the Welsh 'Plas Cadwgan' which means 'Cadogan's Hall' as a 'Place . . . called Cadogan'. Plas Cadwgan was in fact a magnificent late medieval stone-built house only demolished some ten years ago. It was sited on the western side of Wrexham in Denbighshire in what is today the County of Clwyd. At the time of Cadogan's letter the house was in the ownership of the Myddleton family and had been since the early seventeenth century. In view of its antiquity it is nonetheless quite possible that at one time the house was in possession of a member of the Cadogan family. It is also interesting that when the family name is taken as the Peerage title, it is more usual in the case of Earldoms to omit the word 'of'. For whatever reason, however, the word 'of' appears in Cadogan's Letters Patent although thereafter he is generally referred to simply as 'Earl Cadogan'.

Cadogan was once again at the Hague on the 15th May and on the 4th June, acting as His Majesty's Ambassador, he called at the Binnenhof, seat of Dutch government, to inform the Chairman of the States General of his intention to make a formal public entry into the town on the 8th June. He would go to Delft on the morning of that day and then travel to the Hague by water. The Chairman's Steward was instructed to make arrangements for Cadogan's reception at Delft and for his subsequent journey to Hoornbrug near to the Hague where he would be met by two Deputies arriving in the State Coach drawn by six horses followed by a considerable number of other coaches drawn by six, four or two horses depending upon the occupants' rank. Eight further Deputies were instructed to welcome Cadogan on his arrival at the Binnenhof and to dine with him in the evenings. All went according to plan and at half-past-twelve in the afternoon of the 8th June, Cadogan was led by the Burgomaster of Delft to the yacht in which he was to sail to the Hague. Cadogan's aide had made all the preparations for his landing at Hoornbrug and during the reception committee's drive from the Hague outriders were sent to check on the yacht's progress to ensure that the party's arrival at the quayside coincided with that of Cadogan's. The arrangements worked smoothly and following dis-embarkation the procession was formed. Cadogan's retinue consisted, in order, of two Swiss 'guards' and twenty-four footmen walking two abreast with their hats on, Cadogan's aide and twelve pages all on horseback, twelve noblemen mounted, the Ambassador's coach drawn by eight horses and finally three other coaches each drawn by six horses and carrying Cadogan's secretary, chaplains and 'other domestics'.

On arrival at the Hague, the Deputies escorted Cadogan to the house of Prince Maurice of Orange, called the Mauritshuis, which was to be his residence for the period of his stay as the guest of the States General. The eight other

The Mauritshuis

Honours and a Formal Entry

Deputies were now sent to welcome him and subsequently 'keep him company' at dinner. Strict attention was paid to protocol and throughout his stay at the Mauritshuis Cadogan, when entertaining, was punctilious in ensuring that the Deputies all sat in chairs with arms while he sat at the lower end of the table and that, afterwards, he escorted them to their coaches 'on his right side'. When, however, the Deputies hosted Cadogan he was seated in the place of honour in a red velvet chair with a cushion while they had chairs without arms. There were many toasts to be proposed on these occasions. The State Steward would toast King

The Binnenhof

George whereupon Cadogan would raise his glass to their High Mightinesses the States General. Toasts were then made to the Prince and Princess of Wales and other princes and princesses of the blood, to Cadogan, to the concord between Great Britain and the States General and finally to each one of the Deputies present that evening. There was musical accompaniment at dinner and on each occasion when Cadogan or one of the Deputies entered or departed from the Mauritshuis, trumpeters stationed at the windows sounded a fanfare.

On the 10th June Cadogan requested a public audience with their High Mightinesses and this was granted for the following day. At the time arranged a procession was formed similar to the one which accompanied Cadogan's entry and he then progressed with all due ceremony the short distance from the Mauritshuis to the Binnenhof where, as he descended from his coach, he was met by a roll of drums and a guard of honour. Cadogan and his staff were then led by two Deputies to the First Chamber which was lined by pages and noblemen. He then entered the main Council Chamber where, after much bowing on both sides, he was seated on a velvet chair opposite the Presiding Deputy. Cadogan then put on his hat and when 'the great multitude of spectators had been silenced', he addressed the President in French. The President replied in the same language and whenever, during the speeches, mention was made of King George or the States General, 'all present bared their heads'. The audience then came to an end and Cadogan was escorted to his coach for the return procession to the Mauritshuis.

The following day Cadogan returned to his embassy

An ambassador's entry procession into the Hague 1714

and reported to London that 'I, Lord Cadogan, had my
public audience of the States with the usual honours and
solemnity. I gave them the assurances of His Majestys
friendship and of his resolution to maintain an entire union
with this Republick.' Cadogan's public entry to the Hague
'was the most splendid and magnificent appearance that had
been beheld there and judged by all to be of a noble and
beautiful contrivance.'[6]

CHAPTER X

Of Caversham and a Dowry

In the month of April 1718 Lord Cadogan acquired the freehold interest of his Caversham estate from the trustees of the Earl of Kildare for £6200.[1] A Private Act of Parliament was necessary, due to the Earl having bequeathed a life interest in this and other properties to the Duke of Richmond, a natural son of Charles II by the Duchess of Portsmouth. Cadogan now set about building a new mansion house 'commensurate with the magnificence of his prospects' and also landscaping the parkland. He entered into an agreement with a Newbury gardener for the making of parterres, terrace walks with two canals, kitchen gardens and orchards for the sum of £836.7s.11d.[2] While these works were in progress Cadogan returned to the Continent and, following his formal entry to the Hague, he was busily engaged for some months there and in Brussels in negotiations with the Imperial ministers and the Dutch representatives relevant to the working of the Barrier Treaty. He was also much occupied in the negotiations for a Quadruple Alliance between Great Britain, France, Austria and the States General. In one of his reports written during the month of June he describes the 'negotiating this affair' as being more troublesome than 'soliciting the House of Commons'. The object of the Alliance was to guarantee the treaty of Utrecht by settling the conflicting claims of Spain and the Empire in Italy.

Cadogan returned to London at the end of January 1719 and remained for five months. During his stay, on the 5th May, he entered into a contract with the Duke of Richmond whereby, for a consideration of £60,000 payable within three years, the Duke agreed that his son and heir the Earl of March, a grandson of Charles II, would marry Cadogan's elder daughter Lady Sarah Cadogan. The consideration or dowry was over and above a further payment of £20,000 and Cadogan was required to enter into a collateral agreement that in the event of his defaulting he would be liable to pay a penalty of £100,000. The money paid by Cadogan was to be used for the 'purchase of Lands Tenements or Hereditaments in England of an Estate in Fee Simple (Freehold) which when purchased should be settled' on the young couple and their heirs.[3] At the time of the marriage contract Lady Sarah was twelve years old while Lord March was thirteen days short of his eighteenth birthday. Legend has it that the agreement for the marriage came about as the result of a gambling debt owed by the Duke to Cadogan, presumably on the basis that the marriage would cancel the debt. Cadogan's proclivity towards the gaming tables certainly lends credence to the story. The marriage took place at the Hague on the 4th December 1719 and immediately thereafter Lady March was returned to her parents while Lord March left for a Grand Tour of the European capitals in the company of a tutor.

Cadogan had arrived back at the Hague some five months earlier, at the end of June, and until the time of Lady Sarah's marriage he was again much preoccupied with the arrangements for the Quadruple Alliance. On the 20th February 1720 another family matter called for his attention and he wrote to Lord Townshend,

I must on this occasion beg leave to recommend my nephew Sir Thomas Prendergast [whose father had been killed at Malplaquet] to your Lordships favours. He has a cause before the House of Lords which I am persuaded will be found a very just one, and as far as it is so I entreat your Lordship to countenance it. His adversary is a cunning knavish lawyer who tho a most zealous Jacobite and a Papist has however found means to be so strongly supported, that unless your Lordship and my friends attend the hearing my nephews cause notwithstanding the justice of it may chance to suffer.[4]

His family duty done Cadogan now travelled to Vienna accompanied by his brother for the formal signing of the Quadruple Alliance and later in the year he returned to the Hague.

The 2nd Viscount Townshend

Of Caversham and a Dowry

At about this time Cadogan's new mansion house at Caversham was completed at a cost, reputedly, of £130,000. Presumably to assist him in his financial affairs Cadogan sold his house in Dublin, once the home of his grandfather Major William Cadogan, and his estate in County Meath to his cousin Lord Shelburne for £4255.[5] The sale took place on the 17th April 1719. Less than two years later he sold Castle Adare and 473 acres of his estate in County Limerick for £3157.[6] Although no detailed elevational drawings or paintings have survived, Caversham was by all accounts a magnificent house. It appears to have had three storeys with a central frontage of some 250 feet and has been likened to Cliveden. Colin Campbell, the eighteenth-century Palladian architect, prepared a plan of Caversham in 1725 and wrote of it that

The situation is very high, but the assent so easy and gradual, that you rise insensibly to it; where the eye is entertained with most beautiful prospects; particularly that from the grand terras, 1200 feet long, towards Reading and the Thames. The descent from the terras to the bottom of the parterre, is 50 feet perpendicular, by two double flights of steps, all of Portland stone. The parterre is nobly adorned with fountains, vases and statues, particularly four originals in statuary marble, of King William, King George, Duke of Marlborough, and Prince Eugene, all so very like, that they are known at sight; besides many valuable ones cast from the best Antiques. On each side of the parterre, are two great canals 900 feet long, with a Dorick portico at each end. From the great iron gates, to the end of the Park pale, are four beautiful lawns, divided by three walks of very lofty trees, 2200 feet long, and the whole Park is well wooded, watered, and plenty of deer, a pheasantry, menagerie, and all manner of conveniences. This noble Lord [Cadogan], from a place that could pretend to nothing but a situation capable of improvement, with vast labour and expense, has now rendered it one of the noblest seats in the Kingdom.[7]

[109]

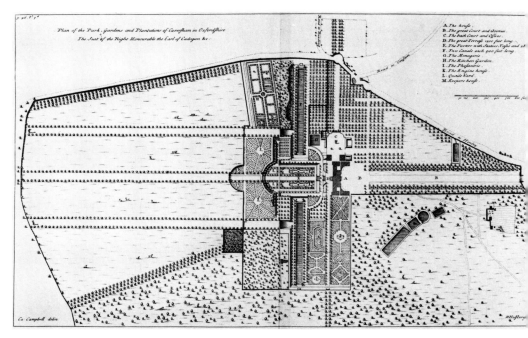

Plan of Caversham Park

Caversham was not, however, entirely without its problems for Cadogan and on the 1st January and again in July 1722 the great deer-park was raided by armed and mounted men who slaughtered sixteen fallow deer.[8] In the main, though, Cadogan must have been content with 'his own variant of Blenheim Palace'.

On the 20th February 1722, Cadogan was appointed Master Surveyor of the Ordnance with a remuneration of £300 per annum. The event, however, that was causing most excitement in the Cadogan household at this time was the expected return of Lord March from his Grand Tour. No doubt Cadogan was now given to wondering as to the compatability of his daughter and son-in-law. On the 22nd April o.s. Cadogan, perhaps displaying a little anxiety, wrote from London to Lord March:

[110]

Of Caversham and a Dowry

My Dear Lord,

I was extremely glad to find by your Lordships letter of the 21st of this month N.S. that you were safely arrived at Luneville, and I hope to have very soon the pleasure of seeing you in Holland. I design to embark the latter end of this week, and as soon as I get to the Hague, I shall give your Lordship immediate notice, and expect you there with impatience. The King goes the 16th May o.s. so that your Lordship will have an opportunity to wait on him as he passes thro Holland, and you may come for England with Lady March afterwards in the yatch that has carried his Majesty over. My Lady Duchess [Lord March's mother] intends to be in Town about that time to meet your Lordship and Lady March, and Her Grace and I have agreed, that you shall pass part of the Summer att Goodwood [the Richmond's home] and part at Causham [Caversham]. I doubt not Her Grace has given your Lordship a particular account of this plan wee have formed for you, so that I shall add nothing more but my best and sincerest wishes for the continuance of your Lordships health, and I am my Dear Lord,

Your most obedient and most
Faithful Humble Servant
CADOGAN

My most humble services to Mr. Hill [Lord March's tutor], I believe he is not a little pleased to have got so near home.[9]

Shortly afterwards Lord March arrived at the Hague and, if another legend is to be believed, he 'was in no great hurry to resume relations with the poor little bride of whom he had nought but the distasteful recollections occasioned by the sordid circumstances of their union. And so, instead, he repaired to the theatre, intending to spend what he bitterly imagined to be his remaining hours of happiness in the enjoyment of the drama.' Lo and behold, at the theatre he espied a 'beauteous lady with whom he promptly fell over head and ears in love at first sight.'[10] In response to Lord

March's fevered enquiries it transpired that the young lady was none other than the reigning toast, the beautiful Lady March. Cadogan need not have worried. All was well. There is perhaps a note of fatherly relief in his next letter to Lord March dated the 5th June o.s:

My Dear Lord,
I most heartily congratulate your Lordship and my Daughter on your safe arrival in Holland, and hope to have very soon the pleasure of seeing you both here. I conclude that before this can get to you, your Lordship will have returned all the civilitys and visits you received on the occasion which brought you to Raphorst, I therefore desire your Lordship would lose no time in coming to England, for besides the infinite impatience of your friends here to see you, the King designs to review the Horse Guards towards the latter end of this month, and it will be extremely right for your Lordship to be then present. In case my wife should think it necessary for your Lordship to make a short visit to her relations att Amsterdam, four or five days will be sufficient for it, and my Lady Duchess is of opinion with me this ceremony should not be omitted, if your Lordship finds tis expected, or will be kindly taken. This small delay Her Grace has consented to but hopes your Lordship will not stay longer on any account, in which I heartily joyn with her. I want words my dear Lord to express how desirous I am to see you and Lady March, and how much I wish your happiness and prosperity. I am my Lord . . . [etc]

CADOGAN

I have taken care to pay all the bills your Lordship has drawn on me.[11]

Cadogan's old friend and patron the Duke of Marlborough died at his home at Windsor Lodge on the 16th June 1722 aged 72 years. He had suffered a paralytic stroke in May 1716 and another six months later which left him with a speech impediment. The Duke nonetheless continued to attend the House of Lords until November 1721, when his health began to fail. With Marlborough's death Cadogan, who was thought by the King to be 'the best officer in England, and the most capable of commanding the army,'[12] succeeded to the posts of Commander-in-Chief of the army and Master-General of the Ordnance. He also became Colonel of the First Foot Guards (The Grenadier Guards) from the 18th June and he was appointed a Commissioner of Chelsea Hospital. On the 9th August the Duke of Marlborough was interred in the Duke of Ormonde's vault in Westminster Abbey with much martial pomp and in the funeral procession Cadogan led a group of high officers who had fought with Marlborough in the Spanish War.

Soon afterwards there came a revival of Jacobite plots with schemes for tampering with the Tower garrison and 'seizing on the Tower and Bank'.[13] The King postponed a visit to Hanover and retired to Kensington Palace under the protection of Cadogan who took personal command of a force comprising seven battalions of Foot Guards, four troops of Horse Guards and two troops of Grenadier Guards all encamped at nearby Hyde Park. The crisis was over by November and the camp was broken up. The King was then able to embark for Hanover and in his absence Cadogan was appointed one of the Lords Justices of the Realm. Cadogan in his fifty-first year was now at the pinnacle of his power.

CHAPTER XI

Return to Westminster

As the Duke of Marlborough's health had declined the Duchess had taken an increasing interest in his finances. It will be remembered that, prior to his going into exile in 1712, Marlborough had sent £50,000 to Cadogan at the Hague and this money Cadogan, as the Duke's agent, invested in Dutch government funds paying 2½ per cent interest. Cadogan then transferred the investment into Austrian loans which paid 8 per cent, a handsome increase in return for the Duke's emergency fund. After a time, however, the Austrian securities fell heavily in market value with the result that the Duke suffered a financial loss. Cadogan's gamble with the higher risk securities had failed. No doubt had the Duke been in sound health and in charge of his own affairs the matter would have been resolved amicably between the two old campaigners but unfortunately, and unknown to the Duke, the 'avaricious'[1] Sarah intervened and made 'outrageous accusations against Marlborough's friend as if he was a common thief'.[2] Sarah's antagonism towards Cadogan, which perhaps was sparked by jealousy at his close friendship with the Duke, resulted in a law suit in which the Duchess was successful 'and Marlborough's brave and faithful comrade, always lax in money matters, had great difficulty in making the necessary restitution'.[3]

[114]

Sarah Churchill,
Duchess of Marlborough

James Brydges, 1st Duke of Chandos

For Cadogan the result of Sarah's action came at a difficult time as, after spending a huge sum on Caversham, he had still to pay Lady March's dowry. Fortunately his son-in-law, now the 2nd Duke of Richmond following his father's death on the 27th May 1723, agreed on the 6th June to Cadogan having a further three years in which to pay the £60,000.

Cadogan's few remaining years are best discovered in his letters to the Duke of Richmond. He writes from London on the 22nd October (o.s.) 1723:

MY DEAR LORD

I am extremely obliged to your Grace for your letter of the 26th Instant n.s. from the Hague. It gave me the double satisfaction of knowing that you were safely arrived there, and that you intended to come very soon for England. I thank your Grace for the particular detail you sent of the

[115]

state of the Duchess of Portsmouths affairs [the Duchess was the Duke's grandmother] and I find your journey to France was absolutely necessary. Before your Grace leaves The Hague Lord Canarvon will very probably be there. The Duke of Chandos has proposed him for Lady Margaret [Cadogan's younger daughter] and offers such conditions as I doe not dislike. I shall not however resolve positively on any thing, till I see your Grace. I must beg of you to be particularly civil to him, and to find out his inclinations in relation to Whig and Tory, for should he have any tendency towards being the latter, I shall think no more of the match. The Prince and Princess [of Wales] are to come to Town on Saturday next. There is no manner of news. I hope the Duchess of Richmond is perfectly recovered of her indisposition and I am My Dear Lord, with the greatest regard and Esteem,

Your most obedient and most
Faithful Humble Servant
CADOGAN

My most humble services to Lord and Lady Albemarle [the Duke's brother-in-law and sister Anne].[4]

The proposed marriage of Lady Margaret Cadogan to Lord Carnarvon did not materialise due to some difference of opinion between the two fathers on the question of a dowry. Lady Margaret eventually married Count Bentinck, fourth son of the 1st Earl of Portland. The Duke of Chandos before his enoblement was James Brydges, the Paymaster of the Forces Abroad and well known to Cadogan from his time as Marlborough's Quartermaster-General and their shared schooldays at Westminster.

Cadogan's next letter to have survived is dated the 1st August 1724, again from London:

MY DEAR LORD

I have this minute received the Honour of your Grace's letter dated yesterday. I beg you to beleive that if some business of moment had not indispensably obliged me to be here on Thursday, I should have stayed att Goodwood till your Grace went from thence. I hope I need not assure you that I am never so happy nor so easy, as when I am with your Grace and Dear Lady Dutchess. I have accepted your bill to Major Gardner before I received your letter, and your Grace may depend upon it, that I shall accept whatever bills you may have occasion to draw on me. I got safe to Town before it was dark on Tuesday and was, God be thanked, very well that day, but yesterday I had a violent feaverish fit which lasted a great while. Sir Hans Sloane [Charles Cadogan's father-in-law] ordered me the Bark [quinine] of which I have taken already no small quantity. I find myself much better today and was att Court tho I have still a Pain in my head which makes writing uneasy to me, and must excuse this scrawl which I am afraid you will be hardly able to read. My blessing to Lady Dutchess and humble services to all the good Company with you. I am My Dear Lord . . . etc.[5]

CADOGAN

Three weeks pass before Cadogan writes again. On this occasion the letter comes from Caversham and is dated the 20th August:

MY LORD

I received yesterday the honour of your Graces of the 18th. I design to review your Regiment the first of next month, and to goe the day before to Hackwood. I write to morrow to the Duke of Bolton [Lord-Lieutenant of Hampshire and Dorset] who is now att Burly in the [New] Forrest, to acquaint him of it. If anything should happen to delay the review, I shall take care to let your Grace know it in time. I am extremely glad that you intend me the favour of coming To Causham [Caversham] as soon as the review is over. I wish Mr. Cambel could order his business so as to be here att the same time. I am rejoyced to find that the Dutchess continues in good health, my blessing to her and a thousand assurances of my tenderest friendship. I am sorry the review falls out so near the time she expects to lye in, but your Grace is not absolutely obliged to be there and I am certain the Duke of Bolton will dispense with your coming as well my self, so that your Grace needs not be under any constraint as to that point. My sister Pendergast [wife of the late Sir Thomas Prendergast] is to be att London in a very few days, and she will be as assisting as she can to the Dutchess. I goe three times a week to Windsor, so that I allmost live upon the road. The King is most extremely delighted with the place, and talks of making a garden below the terrace. I am My Dear Lord . . . etc.[6]   CADOGAN

There is then an interval of some eight and half months before Cadogan's next letter from London dated the 1st May 1725:

MY DEAR LORD

I received last night the honour of your Graces letter from Hersham, and if any thing could add to the affection friendship and esteem I have for you, it would be your interesting your self so warmly and so generously in every thing which relates to me. I cannot better explain to your Grace my present situation than by transmitting here enclosed the letter I received from Lord Townshend [now President of Council] to signify my dismission from the ordnance, to which I may add, that it was the utmost reluctancy that the King consented to my removal. The Duke of Argyle is to have nothing to doe with the command of the army, and tho the Duke of Bolton is made the Constable of the Tower, he however keeps his Regiment. His Majesty having declared, that the Duke of Argyle shall neither have that Regiment nor any other. I send back your Graces Commissions, but shall ever retain the most lively sense of your kind intentions to have parted with them on my account, and I am not so rebuted by the present stroke, but that I still hope and beleive, I shall have it one day in my Power to shew my gratitude by some thing more solid than thanks, which in the mean while I beg your Grace to accept of. I design to goe to Causham the day after the King embarks. I desire your Grace to assure Lady Dutchess of my most tender affections, and to beleive that I have the Honour to be with the most sincere Esteem and Respect my Dear Lord . . . etc

CADOGAN

Your Grace will send back Lord Townshends letter[7]

[118]

Sarah (née Cadogan) Duchess of Richmond with her husband the 2nd Duke of Richmond

Cadogan's 'dismission' from his appointment as Master-General of the Ordnance came about as the result of some factional struggle within the Whig ministry. In the event, and this must have been a bitter blow to Cadogan, the Duke of Argyle did succeed him as Commander-in-Chief of the army. Lord Townshend's letter has not survived.

An invalid Cadogan then writes to his son-in-law from Caversham on the 15th July:

MY DEAR LORD

Tho my being still obliged to keep my bed makes writing a little uneasy, yet I could not refuse my self the pleasure of thanking you by the very first opportunity for your kind and obliging letter of the 13th. I continue God be thanked to grow better and better, and the surgeons say I recover as fast as ever any body did after so severe an operation. I

[119]

am extremely glad to find by your Graces letter, that I shall have the satisfaction to see you here with Lady Dutchess the beginning of next month. If Mr Hill has no engagement att that time I hope he will come with your Grace. He may be assured of a hearty welcome, an easy chair and Tokay [a rich, sweet, aromatic Hungarian wine]. My most humble services to the good company with you. When I write next to Prince Eugene I shall not fail to recommend Faustina [a celebrated singer of the day] in the manner you desire. I rejoyce to hear that she is engaged by our Royal Academy of Musique after she leaves Vienna, tis a most important piece of good news, and must raise considerably the opera actions, which as I take it, ought to be as much the case and concern of the Publick as those in Exchange Ally. I am afraid your Grace will be hardly able to read this scrawl. I am forced to write it in twenty different positions and none of them very easy. I am My Dear Lord . . . etc.[8]

CADOGAN

Come the 14th September and Cadogan is still invalided at Caversham. He writes to the Duke:

Faustina Bordoni, the famous Venetian prima donna

Return to Westminster

My Dear Lord

I received yesterday in the afternoon your Graces letter by your running footman and am infinitely obliged to you for your kind enquiry and concern about my health. I have been extremely ill since the last operation, of the stone cholic, but am now God be praised very easy, and my wound begins to mend tho slowly. I rest well, and have a good strength and am allowed to eat a chicken every day. What retards the cure is a sharp kumour [tumour] that falls upon the wound, and to dry up this kumour the surgeons use all outward and inward means, which begin to have in some measure their effect, for it lessens every day. I writt to your Grace by last thursdays post and directed Le Blanc to wait on you yesterday in his way to London. Little Caroline [the Duke's two-year-old daughter] is mighty well and amuses me extremely. Assure Lady Dutchess of my most tender affection. I have received a letter from her, which I shall answer by next post. My most humble Services to Lord and Lady Albemarle. I am . . . etc.

CADOGAN

I shall take care of the Four hundred Pounds your Grace sayes L'abbe will want. It shall be ready about three weeks after michaelmas.[9]

Five days later Cadogan wrote his final letter of the series to the Duke, again from Caversham:

My Dear Lord

Since my writing last to your Grace, I have God be thanked mended a good deal, and as Sir Hans Sloane and Mr. Busiere are of opinion I should hasten to London, to have their advice and assistance in case of accidents, I design to goe there as soon as I can bear the jolting of a coach, which if the wound continues to heal as it has done of late, will I hope be in a very few days. When I can fix the time, I shall let your Grace know it. Little Caroline is in perfect health she will goe in the coach with my nieces. My Brother and Sister came here on thursday last, they desire your Grace to accept of their respects. My most humble services to Lord and Lady Albemarle. I am my dear Lord . . . etc.

CADOGAN[10]

Cadogan did not recover from his operation and less than a year later, on the 17th July 1726, he died during a stay at the fashionable village of Kensington Gravel Pits. He was 54 years old. 'The Earl Cadogan dyed in top dress and kept on him to the last his great wig, imbroydered coat, brocade vest, red top shoes, diamond buckles . . .' He was buried four days later, at night as was then not unusual, in the Duke of Ormonde's vault in King Henry VII's chapel in Westminster Abbey, taking his place for the last time at Marlborough's side.

In 1724 The French ambassador reported that 'the immense wealth he (Cadogan) has acquired, and his having, by means of the powerful influence of the Duke of Marlborough, passed over the head of many of his seniors in the army, have drawn upon him a great many enemies.'[11] This was certainly so and is perhaps evidenced by comments at the time of Marlborough's funeral in 1722 when his detractors accused him of appearing 'indecorously dressed and betraying his want of sympathy by his looks and gestures'.[12] The occasion also gave rise to some savage lines by the Jacobite Bishop of Rochester, an erstwhile occupant of the Tower who, said Cadogan, should be 'flung to the lions':[13]

> Unmoved by Mercy and by Shame unaw'd,
> Th' undoubted spawn of Hangman and of Bawd:
> Ungrateful to th' ungrateful man he grew by,
> A bawling blustering boystrous bloody booby[14]

Others have treated Cadogan with greater perception and one commentator writing in 1800 has said that Cadogan was 'frank, open, vehement, impatient of contradiction,

rather to cut the gordian knot with his sword, than attempt
by patience to unravel its intricacy'.[15] Sir Winston Churchill,
a descendant of the Duke of Marlborough, writing in more
recent years of the Duke's life, describes Cadogan as that
'brave, generous Irish soldier, who was never found wanting
in fidelity or chivalry'.[16] A more recent view of Cadogan
the soldier is that he was a 'brilliant staff officer . . . worth
his weight in gold'.[17]

Critics of Cadogan have branded him a 'thief'[18] and
certainly he used his office as Marlborough's Quartermaster-
General to amass great wealth. He did this by wagering on
the course of the war and by taking a profit on the currency
dealing that was necessary to pay the troops.[19] In Cadogan's
day such means of gain were looked upon as legitimate
perquisites of office in much the same category as Marlborough's percentage on the bread money. James Brydges,
the first Duke of Chandos and Paymaster of the Forces
Abroad during the War of the Spanish Succession is reputed
to have made £600,000 out of his office.[20] 'Autres temps,
autre moeurs.'

It has been written of Marlborough that 'England never
produced a greater soldier',[21] and his greatness is generally
related to the Allied victories at Blenheim, Ramillies,
Oudenarde and Malplaquet which did much to raise
Britain into the position of a world power. But would
Marlborough, who suffered from indifferent health,[22] have
been so successful without the 'efficiency and daring' and
'brilliant organisation'[23] of his Quartermaster-General?
Perhaps not. The Earl of Strafford (formerly Lord Raby),
writing early in 1713 to the Lord Treasurer, stated that 'I do
believe the greatest part of Lord Marlborough's victories

are owing to him [Cadogan] and even the Pensionary [First Minister of Holland] said to me "Si vous voulez avoir un duc de Marlborough un Cadogan est Necessaire".' One of Cadogan's critics has said that he was 'one of the true victors of Marlborough's wars'.[24] Marlborough was a gifted leader of men in battle. Cadogan in his own right was a great soldier, not to be lost in Marlborough's shadow.

Epilogue

Cadogan died without a male heir and the title of Baron of Oakley passed to his brother Charles. The new Lord Cadogan, together with Lord Shelburne (his cousin) and Lord Carteret (another 'Old Westminster'), were appointed executors under the First Earl's will and they had the unenviable task of ordering his financial affairs. At the time of his death the Duchess of Richmond's dowry of £60,000 was unpaid and accordingly on the 11th July 1727 the Duke and Duchess obtained an Order from the Court of Chancery directing that the executors sell off the late Earl's real and personal estate 'not specifically devised'[1] to satisfy the debt. The dowry was eventually paid and part of this was achieved by the 2nd Baron purchasing the Caversham estate where he lived until his death in 1776 in his 92nd year. Caversham was sold by the 3rd Baron Cadogan in 1783. The Manor of Oakley was sold by the 2nd Baron to Sarah, Dowager Duchess of Marlborough in 1730. Following Sarah's death in 1744, the Duke's coffin was removed from Westminster Abbey and both were then buried in the chapel at Blenheim Palace.

The 1st Earl's wife continued to live at Raaphorst until her death in 1749 when she was buried in Holland. There was then some dispute between Lady Bentinck, Cadogan's

younger daughter, and Cadogan's executors and this resulted in the property being sold in 1754 and the proceeds
being sent to England for a final distribution between the
First Earl's creditors.

The marriage of the Duke and Duchess of Richmond
proved to be 'exceptionally happy' and the Duchess became
pregnant twenty-seven times, bearing the Duke twelve
children.[2] The Duke died on the 8th August 1750 while the
Duchess 'died of grief for his loss'[3] just over a year later on
the 25th August 1751. 'Little Caroline' Lennox, the Richmond's eldest daughter, shocked London society when she
was 21, by eloping with Henry Fox, later Lord Holland.
She subsequently married him against her parents' wishes
and died in 1777.

Cadogan's old friend Lord Raby, who became the 3rd
Earl of Strafford, died 'of the stone'[4] at Wentworth Castle
on the 15th November 1739 in his 68th year.

In 1777 the 3rd Baron Cadogan, later to become the 1st
Earl Cadogan of the new creation, married Mary Churchill, a kinswoman of the Duke of Marlborough, so uniting
the two ancient families. The bond was strengthened in
1920 when Alexandra Mary Cadogan, a grand-daughter of
the 5th Earl Cadogan, married the 10th Duke of Marlborough. Their eldest son John is the present Duke.

The 1st Earl Cadogan
(1672–1726)
Last Will & Testament

In the Name of God Amen – I William Earl Cadogan do hereby revoke annul and make void all former Wills by me at any time heretofore made and do make this my last Will and Testament that is to say I do ratify and confirm the articles of agreement I executed with the late Duke of Richmond upon the marriage of his son and my Daughter the now Duke and Duchess of Richmond and I do also ratify and confirm the settlement I made upon my brother Colonel Charles Cadogan at the time of his marriage.

Item my mind and will is that if my said son and daughter the Duke and Duchess of Richmond shall claim demand and recover any part of my estate in Holland by reason of any of the laws or customs there that the same shall be made good and reimbursed to my estate in Holland out of the monies and estate I agreed to pay and settle on the marriage of my said son and daughter Richmond and I do give to my youngest daughter the Lady Margaret Cadogan and her children all such monies which shall be so reimbursed and for want of issue of my said youngest daughter I give the same to my said brother his heirs and executors.

Item my mind and will is that whatever Estate I have or am entitled unto after the several deceases of my said son and daughter the Duke and Duchess of Richmond without issue of their bodies by or virtue of the said marriage articles I do give devise and bequeath the same to my said youngest daughter and her issue and for want of such issue to my said brother his heirs and executors.

Item I do give and bequeath unto my five nieces daughters of my sister Dame Penelope Prendergast one thousand pounds a piece to be paid out of the debt which my nephew Sir Thomas Prendergast Baronet owes me and the remainder of the said debt I give and release to him he ratifying and making good to his mother her joynture and paying all sums of money he now owes and shall owe her.

Item I given to my said youngest daughter Margaret the sum of eight thousand pounds out of my estate in Holland and I give to my wife during her life the enjoyment of the remainder of all my real and personal estate in Holland not herein before disposed of and then I give the same to my said youngest daughter and her children and in default of such issue then to my said daughter the Duchess of Richmond and her children and in default of issue then to my said brother and in default of his issue then to the said Sir Thomas Prendergast his heirs and executors.

Item I give to my said sister the Lady Prendergast and her executors my house in Jermyn Street and also my house in Piccadilly now let to Mr. Dearing and also the sum of one thousand five hundred pounds of lawful money of Great Britain.

Item I will that my executors hereinafter named shall lay out fifty pounds to buy a communion plate for the use of the Church of Caversham in Oxfordshire.

Item I give all my family pictures to the said Duke of Richmond.

Item I do give devise and bequeath unto the Right Honourable the Earl of Shelburn the Lord Carteret and my said Brother Colonel Cadogan their heirs and executors and administrators all my manors houses lands tenements and hereditaments with their and every of their appurtenances in England and also my plate jewels household goods and personal estate whatsoever not herein before disposed of in trust that they shall sell and dispose of the same and by and out of the monies to be raised by such sale or sales pay and satisfy in the first place all such sums of money as I am engaged or have agreed or covenanted to pay by virtue of the said articles executed by me upon the said marriage of my said son and daughter Richmond and then to pay and satisfy all other my just debts and funeral charges and out of the residue and overplus the rest I do give to my said youngest daughter the sum of twelve thousand pounds and the remainder thereof shall be vested in lands to the use of my said youngest daughter and the heirs of her body and for want of such issue to my said brother and his heirs and I do appoint my executors hereafter named to be likewise trustees for securing and laying out the sum of money agreed by the said articles made on the marriage of the said Duke and Duchess of Richmond to be paid by me according to the true intent and meaning of the said articles and I desire that the said Duke of Richmond may have the preference in the purchase of any part of my said real and personal estate devised to be sold as aforesaid and I desire my entry coach in Holland may be sold and the monies arising thereby may be paid to my said executors upon the trusts herein before mentioned.

Item I do give and devise to my servant Francis Bland who has attended upon me in my present illness the annual sum of forty pounds to be paid him quarterly at the four usual feasts or days of payment in the year during his life without any deduction or abatement whatsoever the first payment to be made at such of the said feasts as shall next happen after my decease and I also give him the sum of one hundred pounds and I give to each of my menial servants six months of their yearly wages over and above what shall be due to them respectively at my decease and I lastly do make and constitute the said Lord Shelburn Lord Carteret and brother Cadogan Executors of this my last will and testament upon the trusts herein before mentioned and desire to be buried with all the privacy imaginable and not above one hundred and fifty pounds be expended in and about my funeral. In witness whereof I here unto set my hand and seal this twenty seventh day of June in the twelfth year of the Reign of his present Majesty King George anno Dom One thousand seven hundred and twenty six. CADOGAN

Signed sealed and published by the said Earl Cadogan in our presence who have in his presence attested the same and subscribed our names.

J Hancock
Cornet Charles Sanderson

Notes and References

FOREWORD

1 Virginia Cowles, *The Great Marlborough and his Duchess*, p.205.

CHAPTER III

1 Edith R. Curtis, *Lady Sarah Lennox*, p.13.
2 Cited by W.S. Churchill, *Marlborough, his Life and Times*, Vol. 1, p.447 (of the 1967 paperback edition).

CHAPTER IV

1 *Dictionary of National Biography* (hereafter *DNB*).
2 Additional Mss. 22196 8V. M38832 (British Library).
3 Dr Hare's *Journal*, cited by Churchill, op.cit., Vol. 2, p.291.
4 David Chandler, 'Robert Parker and the Compte de Merode-Westerloo', London 1968, p.31.
5 Major the Hon. Ralph Legge-Pomeroy, *The Regimental History of the 5th Dragoon Guards 1685–1922*, p.104.
6 A.S. Turberville, *English Men and Manners in the Eighteenth Century*, p.478.
7 *Treasury Papers* xciii 79, cited in *DNB*.
8 *DNB*.
9 *London Gazette*, 1708 – 4467/4. *Military Dictionary*, 1704.
10 Additional Mss. 22196 33V. M38832.
11 Additional Mss. 22196 46V. M38832.

CHAPTER V

1 PRO London C/54/4981.
2 Churchill, op.cit., Vol. 3, p.203.
3 Additional Mss. 22196 79V. M38832.
4 Additional Mss. 22196 129V. M38832.
5 Sgt. J. Millner, *A Compendious Journal*, London 1733, p.212.
6 David Chandler, *Marlborough as Military Commander*, p.213.

7 Ibid., p.219.
8 T. Lediard, *Life of John, Duke of Marlborough*, London 1736, Vol. 2, p.303.
9 Sir George Murray, *Letters and Despatches of John Churchill, First Duke of Marlborough*, London 1845, Vol. 4, p.144.
10 I.F. Burton, *The Captain-General*, London 1968, p.140, citing Marlborough.

CHAPTER VI

1 J.G. Pelet and F.E. de Vault, *Mémoires militaires relatifs à la succession d'Espagne sous Louis XIV*, Paris 1836–42, Vol. 9, p.86.
2 W. Kane, *Campaigns of King William and Queen Anne 1689–1712*, London 1745, p.851.
3 Legge-Pomeroy, op.cit., p.104.
4 *DNB*.
5 Legge-Pomeroy, op.cit., p.104.
6 Churchill, op.cit., Vol. 4, p.151.
7 Blenheim Collection.
8 Dr Sturgill cited by Chandler, op.cit., p.275.
9 Captain Robert Parker cited by Chandler, op.cit., p.289.
10 Churchill, op.cit., Vol. 4, p.374.
11 A Whig, 'Clerk of Deliveries' during the War of the Spanish Succession and elected to Parliament in 1713, who went on to become Secretary at War and a Principal Secretary of State two years later. He died of smallpox in 1721.
12 Stowe Mss. 246 f.10.

CHAPTER VII

1 Blenheim Collection B2–24.
2 Cited by Churchill, op.cit., 1938 edition, Vol. IV, p.509.
3 Ibid., p.443.
4 Chandler, op.cit., p.306.
5 Richard Cannon, *Historical Record of the 5th Regiment of Dragoon Guards*, p.87.
6 E.P. Thompson, *Whigs & Hunters*, p.100.
7 Cowles, op.cit., p.385.
8 Lease with County Library, Royal County of Berkshire D/EX 258/12.
9 Thompson, op.cit., p.100.

Notes and References

CHAPTER VIII

1 H.W. Meikle, *A Short History of Scotland*, p.294.
2 Blenheim Collection B2–26.
3 Blenheim Collection B2–26.
4 Blenheim Collection B2–26.
5 Blenheim Collection B2–26.
6 Blenheim Collection B2–27.
7 Blenheim Collection B2–27.
8 Blenheim Collection B2–27.
9 Blenheim Collection B2–27.

CHAPTER IX

1 Blenheim Collection B2–26.
2 Collins, *Peerage of England*, 1812, Vol. 5, pp.414–416.
3 *DNB*.
4 M.C. Borer, *The Years of Grandeur*, p.69, citing the *Weekly Medley*, 1717.
5 Collins, op.cit., pp.416–417.
6 Ibid., p.417.

CHAPTER X

1 Agreement in County Library, Royal County of Berkshire D/EX 258/14.
2 Ditto D/EX 258/9.
3 Goodwood Mss. (West Sussex Record Office) 97.
4 Blenheim Collection B2–26.
5 Registry of Deeds, Dublin 23–334–13596.
6 Registry of Deeds, Dublin 36–191–21992.
7 Colin Campbell, *Vitruvius Britannicus*, *c*.1717.
8 Thompson, op.cit., p.100.
9 Goodwood Mss. 106 534.
10 Earl of March, *A Duke and his Friends*, p.64.
11 Goodwod Mss. 106 535.
12 Cited in Thompson, op.cit., p.202.
13 *DNB*.

CHAPTER XI

1 Bryan Bevan, *Marlborough the Man*, p.288.
2 Ibid., p.288.
3 Churchill, op.cit., 1938 edition, Vol. IV, p.513.

4   Goodwood Mss. 106/537.
5   Goodwood Mss. 106/538.
6   Goodwood Mss. 106/539.
7   Goodwood Mss. 106/540.
8   Goodwood Mss. 106/541.
9   Goodwood Mss. 106/542.
10   Goodwood Mss. 106/543.
11   *The House of Commons 1715–1754* (History of Parliment Trust), Vol. I, p.513.
12   *DNB.*
13   W.M. Thackeray, *The Four Georges*, p.32.
14   Cited by Thompson, op.cit., p.203.
15   W. Coxe, *Memoirs of the Life and Administration of Sir Robert Walpole*, p.329.
16   Churchill, op.cit., 1938 edition, Vol. IV, p.578.
17   Cowles, op.cit., pp.165, 200.
18   Van Den Bergh cited in 'The Opening Phase of Marlborough's Campaign of 1708 in the Netherlands', A.J. Veenendaal, *History*, 1950, Vol. 35, p.46.
19   G. Davies, 'The Seamy Side of Marlborough's War', *Huntingdon Library Quarterly*, 1951, Vol. XV, pp.21–44.
20   C.H.C. and M.I. Baker, *Life and Circumstances of James Brydges First Duke of Chandos*, p.xiv.
21   Chandler, op.cit., p.331.
22   Churchill, op.cit., 1938 edition, Vol. IV, p.413 and Chandler, op.cit., p.119.
23   Bevan, op.cit., p.197.
24   Thompson, op.cit., p.100.

                          EPILOGUE
1   Goodwood Mss. 97.
2   A. Foss, *The Dukes of Britain*, p.31.
3   *DNB* entry on Charles Lennox, 2nd Duke of Richmond.
4   *DNB* entry on Thomas Wentworth.

Bibliography

Manuscript Sources

British Library: Additional Manuscripts: 22196 (Cadogan–Raby correspondence), 37371 (Cadogan–Whitworth correspondence), Stowe Manuscripts 228 and 229.
Blenheim Palace: Cadogan–Marlborough correspondence.
West Sussex Record Office: Goodwood Manuscripts (Cadogan–Richmond correspondence).

Printed Sources and Works of Reference

Historical Manuscripts Commission, Polworth Papers and Royal Stuart Papers; *Dictionary of National Biography*; *The Dictionary of Welsh Biography*; Collins' *Peerage of England*.

Authorities Consulted

ENGLAND

Bank of England, Buckinghamshire County Council Record Office, Cheshire County Council Record Office, City of Westminster Archives Department, Goodwood Estate Co. Ltd., H.M. Tower of London, House of Commons Public Information Office, Isle of Wight Record Office, National Army Museum Library, Oxfordshire County Council Record Office, Public Record Office (London), Royal County of Berkshire Library, Shropshire County Council Record Office, The College of Arms, Westminster Abbey Library, Westminster School, West Sussex Record Office.

Bibliography

HOLLAND

Netherlands National Archives, The Hague; Royal Archives, The Hague.

NORTHERN IRELAND

Public Record Office of Northern Ireland, Ulster Historical Foundation.

REPUBLIC OF IRELAND

Christ Church Cathedral, Dublin; Genealogical Office, Dublin Castle; Irish Manuscripts Commission; Meath County Library; National Library of Ireland; Public Record Office of Ireland; Registry of Deeds; Representative Church Body Library, Dublin; Trinity College Library, Dublin; Westmeath County Library.

WALES

Clwyd, Dyfed, Gwent, Gwynedd, and Powys County Council Record Offices; Royal Commission on Ancient and Historical Monuments of Wales; The National Library of Wales.

Published Works

Baker C.H.C. and M.I., *Life and Circumstances of James Bridges First Duke of Chandos*, Oxford at the Clarendon Press 1949.

Barker Ashley, *Notting Hill in Bygone Days*, Anne Bingley 1924.

Bartrum Peter C., *Welsh Genealogies AD 300–1400*, University of Wales Press 1974.

Bartrum Peter C., *Welsh Genealogies AD 1400–1500*, The National Library of Wales 1983.

Bevan Bryan, *Marlborough the Man*, Robert Hale 1975.

Borer M.C., *The Years of Grandeur*, W.H. Allen 1975.

Bottigheimer Karl S., *English Money and Irish Land*, Oxford at the Clarendon Press 1971.

Bradney J.A. Sir, *A History of Monmouthshire*, 1923.

Burtchaell G.D. and T.U. Sadleir, *Alumni Dublinenses*, Alex. Thom, Dublin 1935.

Cannon Richard, *Historical Record of the 5th Regiment of Dragoon Guards*, Longman Orme 1839.

Bibliography

Chandler David, *Marlborough as Military Commander*, B.T. Batsford 1973.

Churchill W.S., *A History of the English Speaking People*, Cassell 1974.

Churchill W.S., *Marlborough His Life and Times*, Harrap 1934/38.

Cowles Virginia, *The Great Marlborough and his Duchess*, Weidenfeld and Nicolson 1983.

Coxe William, *Memoirs of the Life and Administration of Sir Robert Walpole*, 1800.

Crockatt J.H., *John Churchill First Duke of Marlborough*, Quentin Nelson 1970.

Curtis E.R., *Lady Sarah Lennox*, W.H. Allen.

Daiches David, *Charles Edward Stuart*, Thames & Hudson 1973.

Fergusson T.G., *British Military Intelligence 1870–1914*, Arms and Armour Press 1984.

Firth Charles, *Cromwell's Army*, Methuen 1962.

Fletcher C.R.L., *Historical Portraits 1700–1850*, Oxford at the Clarendon Press 1919.

Foss Arthur, *The Dukes of Britain*, The Herbert Press 1986.

Green David, *Blenheim Palace*, Country Life 1951.

Green David, *Sarah Duchess of Marlborough*, Collins 1967.

Gregg Edward, *Queen Anne*, Ark Paperbacks 1984.

Halsband R., *Lord Hervey*, Oxford at the Clarendon Press 1973.

Hamilton Lt.-Gen. Sir F.W., *History of the First or Grenadier Guards*, John Murray 1874.

Hatton R., *George I*, Thames & Hudson 1978.

Ilchester The Countess of and Lord Stavordale, *The Life and Letters of Lady Sarah Lennox 1745–1826*, John Murray 1901.

Kenyon J.P., *Stuart England*, Penguin 1980.

Legge-Pomeroy Major The Hon. R., *The Regimental History of the 5th Dragoon Guards 1685–1922*, Wm. Blackwood Edinburgh 1924.

Lloyd J.E., *A History of Wales*, Longmans, Green 1912.

Macdonald J, *Great Battlefields of the World*, Michael Joseph 1984.

Mackinnon Col. D., *Origin and Services of the Coldstream Guards*, Richard Benley 1833.

McDowell R.B. and D.A. Webb, *Trinity College Dublin 1592–1952*, Cambridge 1982.

March Earl of, *A Duke and his Friends*, Hutchinson 1911.

Bibliography

Meikle H.W., *A Short History of Scotland*, Oliver and Boyd Edinburgh 1951.

Montgomery-Massingberd H., *Blenheim Revisited*, The Bodley Head 1985.

Moody T.W. and Others, *A New History of Ireland*, Oxford at the Clarendon Press 1976.

Pearman R., *The Cadogan Estate*, Haggerston Press 1986.

Plumb J.H., *England in the Eighteenth Century*, Penguin 1981.

Plumb J.H., *Sir Robert Walpole: The Making of a Statesman*, The Cresset Press 1956.

Plumb J.H., *Sir Robert Walpole: The King's Minister*, The Cresset Press 1960.

Plumb J.H., *The First Four Georges*, Fontana/Collins 1983.

Scouller Major R.E., *The Armies of Queen Anne*, Oxford at the Clarendon Press 1966.

Thackeray W.M., *The Four Georges*, Falcon Press 1948.

Thompson E.P., *Whigs & Hunters*, Penguin 1977.

Thomson G.M., *The First Churchill*, Martin Secker & Warburg 1979.

Thorne John and Others, *A History of England*, Ernest Benn 1964.

Trench C.C., *George II*, Allen Lane 1973.

Young G.M., *Macaulay*, Rupert Hart-Davis 1967.

Young Peter, *Oliver Cromwell*, Severn House 1975.

Illustration Acknowledgements

Index

Illustration references are in italic type

Index

Index

Index